Testimonials

"Finally, the concept of Inner Wealth is explored, and there is no one more qualified than Julie Wald for this ambitious undertaking. Not only is Inner Wealth the most critical conversation of our time, Julie Wald is exactly the person to provide us the guidance we need to move from theory to practice."

—NOEL PACARRO BROWN, LEAD OF THE CONSCIOUS WEALTH MANAGEMENT GROUP AT MORGAN STANLEY, CO-HOST OF THE *BETTER MONEY* PODCAST

"Julie Wald is the authentic voice you need to guide, support, and motivate you on your wellness journey. With Inner Wealth, she lays out her health and wellness practice based on her extensive counseling experience and yoga background and gives you the tools you need to make changes big and small in your life. I've had the privilege of knowing Julie for fifteen years, and she is a gifted practitioner who finds a way to meet people where they are and bring them to new heights. A must-read from this brilliant and wise teacher."

—AMY GRIFFIN, FOUNDER OF G9 VENTURES

"Julie Wald's wellness framework is simple, effective, and highly flexible to reflect your personal values and goals."

"Julie Wald is that rare combination of a spiritually developed human being and a great businesswoman. Her new book, Inner Wealth, is built upon her well-established platform of delivering wellness services (yoga, meditation, and the like) to high-performance individuals, integrating inner development with outer achievements, making for a whole and prosperous human being. This kind of integration is right on the cutting edge and is now being sought everywhere—in corporations, entertainment, and fitness companies, among many others. Julie has been well ahead of this curve for many years, and now you can share the secrets of her inner and outer success."

"Knowing Julie Wald for over twenty years, personally and professionally, is a privilege. She embodies every aspect of what it means to live a healthy life, and to feel loved and cared for."

Inner Wealth

INNER
WEALTH

How Wellness Heals,
Nurtures, and Optimizes
Ultra-Successful People

JULIE WALD

STRAWBERRY
FIELDS PRESS

INNER WEALTH

How Wellness Heals, Nurtures, and
Optimizes Ultra-Successful People

ISBN   978-1-5445-0617-3 *Hardcover*

       978-1-5445-0615-9 *Paperback*

       978-1-5445-0616-6 *Ebook*

To my beloved husband and partner in life and work, Michael.

*To my precious children who are my greatest
teachers, Jonah, Eli, and Eviana.*

*I am forever grateful to love you, learn from
you, and walk the earth with you by my side.*

CONTENTS

INTRODUCTION

When I began offering private yoga and meditation lessons to New York's elite, little did I know how far it would take me professionally, that I would fall in platonic love with each and every one of my students, and that my business would grow to a point that I'd want to write a book about my experience. I was in my late twenties, childless, and relatively carefree. I was curious and worked hard to understand why people who seemingly had such abundance were often struggling and unbalanced like the rest of the world. Fast-forward twenty years with a husband, three children, and a demanding business, and some days I feel the same stress and imbalance my clients do—and I'm a wellness advisor and coach. I have learned through my clients and my own personal journey that riding the waves and staying present in our fast-paced, demanding life requires a consistent, compassionate self-care practice.

As I define it, self-care begins when we step into our power, cultivate a compassionate relationship with ourselves, and make the rules for our own life. It's a far more healthy, holistic lifestyle that breeds positive inner feelings than one-off treats such as occasional massages and facials. Self-care affects everyone around us. When we prioritize caring for our mental, physical, and emotional well-being, we show up and express the best version of ourselves for others in our lives. How we treat ourselves also sets the tone for how others will treat us and understand our needs.

THE FOUR PILLARS

Self-care comprises four pillars: movement, stillness, touch, and nourishment. These pillars came to light through the work we have been doing with individuals and families since 2003 at my wellness company, Namaste New York. We witnessed and realized that true well-being does not come from a single magical solution or practice, but rather, it requires a holistic, integrative approach. The four pillars align with the basic ingredients a newborn baby requires for healthy development—and when they're out of balance, our foundation becomes less stable, and like a baby, it becomes more difficult to thrive. We must pay attention to all of the pillars as they are the vital ingredients for a healthy, happy life; if one or two are strong but the rest are wobbly, we lose our balance and can feel unhappy, unwell, and stressed out.

In this book, we'll explore each pillar together, discussing the theory and practices that can help create balance from the inside out and a state of well-being that we all crave and deserve.

MOVEMENT

Our bodies were built to move. Movement helps us develop a sense of skill and invites us to celebrate being alive. Our ancestors moved all day long, yet we've become a sedentary society. Despite evolution, our stress hormones still function from fight-or-flight reaction mode, releasing cortisol and adrenaline, even though we no longer worry about running away from saber-toothed tigers. Centuries ago, escaping from harm released the stress hormones that our bodies adaptively produced in a moment of danger. Today, we're far less likely to have to outrun a predator, but we experience stress that leaves us feeling threatened and vulnerable. What does that mean? The fight-or-flight response is designed to trigger a burst of activity. Movement can calm the nervous system and support the body in breaking down stress hormones so the body can return to homeostasis. Movement also stimulates the body to produce endorphins—those feel-good hormones that make life exponentially more manageable.

In addition to addressing daily stress related to work, family, and relationships, movement becomes particularly important when navigating a major life circumstance or transition such as illness or divorce. Different types of movement can calm us down or lift us up, depending on what we need. Ideally, if we've incorporated movement into our lives before these transitions happen, we're in a better position to face the challenges they bring. Movement is an antidote and can be discovered and incorporated at any time as a tool to help us flourish through more and less challenging chapters in our lives.

We all have our own reasons for prioritizing movement in our lives. For some, it's about longevity, brain health, overall fitness, or a sculpted body. For me, it's about all of those things, but most importantly, I know that yoga and exercise enable me to face my day, help me focus, and put me in a better mood. When my alarm goes off at 5:30 in the morning, a very big part of me wants to press the snooze button. In that moment, if I think about the challenges of the day ahead, and the strength, focus, and calm I will receive from some morning movement, I am able to access the motivation I need to wake up and move. I am less motivated by some abstract idea of health or longevity, and exponentially more inspired by the idea of how movement will help me feel better *today*.

The movement pillar includes practices related to programmed movement, such as fitness and exercise; integrated movement, such as adding movement to our normal routine; and yoga and stretching. Instead of thinking of movement as a chore, I like to think of movement as a celebration and a gift of the human experience.

STILLNESS

In our digital world, there's no question most of us are overstimulated and overworked. We all have a lot to juggle and may work late hours into the night. Even when we are lying in bed or waiting for a train, we are mentally stimulated by the media on our phones. The experience of being in our own skin, feeling our feelings, and listening to and witnessing our thoughts has become a rare occasion for so many people. The flip side of mental and physical movement is stillness—in other words, the companion to work is rest. Our bodies and minds need time for recovery and reflection. A once- or twice-a-year vacation or even weekend downtime isn't enough to make up for the daily stressors of our lives. We need to consistently integrate restorative and relaxing moments throughout our normal routine.

The stillness pillar includes practices of meditation, rest, and reflection. When we slow down, we recalibrate and activate the parasympathetic nervous system so that our bodies and minds can better cope with stress. Stillness is like maternal love for ourselves. It's centering and grounding. It's an opportunity to feel the energy of our own life force and connect with body and mind. If movement is about building strength to face life's challenges, stillness is surrendering to the flow of life in the best possible way.

NOURISHMENT

Nourishment begins with the nutrients we introduce to our bodies. It's not a specific diet per se, as I believe that the food formula is truly different for each of us. It's more about mindfully feeding our bodies with gratitude and joy. And while food is incredibly important, we could be eating the healthiest diet on the planet yet still feel hungry if we are not nourishing our hearts and minds as well. We must make an intentional, concerted effort to partake of art, music, literature, and pure beauty to nourish and stimulate our mind to grow and flex. Likewise, we must fill and expand our hearts with those in our community, and spend time with family and friends to complete the circle of nourishment.

The nourishment pillar includes food to nourish our body, art and natural beauty to nourish our mind, and community to nourish our heart and soul.

TOUCH

Touch speaks to connection, relating and communicating to ourselves and others, and a primal need to be held and supported. On a surface level, connection happens nonverbally, through touch, yet we live in a society that is either deprived or phobic about touch as a way of connecting. We walk about with our phones in our hands instead of holding hands. The language of touch is about giving and receiving, nonverbal communication between two human beings, listening and feeling between "healer" and recipient.

In massage therapy and bodywork, physical touch solicits a deeper, therapeutic exchange between two people, physically and energetically. While community nourishes our being on one level, a deeper connection in a relationship fulfills a primal need for love and true friendship. Lastly, in our digital world, we must be cognizant of how we touch others and how we are touched virtually. The virtual connections that happen online impact our offline connections. This is a new and ever-changing aspect to explore.

The touch pillar includes massage and bodywork, relationships, and plugging into life (and unplugging from everything else).

BRINGING THE FOUR PILLARS INTO YOUR LIFE

For the sake of this book, I present the pillars separately, but they are interwoven. I like to use a cake metaphor when explaining the four pillars and self-care: You always need dry ingredients, wet ingredients, leavening, and sweeteners to make a cake, but the specific ingredients you choose change the cake's flavor and texture. If you use almond flour and coconut oil, your cake will be different than a cake made with wheat flour and butter. Each of the book's four parts focuses on one pillar, but you need all four of them to create a complete recipe for inner wealth.

The pillars are about finding balance between effort and surrender. To stay with our cake metaphor, eggs are part of the cake, but more eggs doesn't always make the cake better. Even when we believe we're taking care of ourselves, we often feel some level of stress and don't understand why. It may be that one of our pillars is weak or that we are overdoing it in a specific realm. For example, someone who exercises five days a week, eats a healthy diet, and has fulfilling relationships with family and friends may still feel depressed or anxious. Of course, real-life factors come into play, but neglecting to take the time for stillness, which involves rest and reflection, could be inhibiting her ability to cope optimally. She could be eating a super-clean diet, but it's so restrictive that she's always eating alone or experiencing stress around food, which can leave her feeling terribly empty.

You're busy; I get that. I am too. Even though it seems like I'm suggesting you add something else to your already packed day, in the long run, these pillars and the practices that bring them to life will support you in navigating the fullness of your life and schedule. The Four Pillars of Wellness are a framework to help you integrate a balanced self-care routine into your days. I'll show you ways to create efficiencies rather than crowd your calendar. We will make moments that already exist more supportive to your health and well-being.

The idea is to engage in four pillar practices from a place of loving yourself and feeling nurtured from the inside out, rather than the perspective of having more to do or the need to be perfect. The lens through which we view the practices impacts our ability to be consistent. You'll find you have more energy, prioritize your time more effectively, and feel healthier if you consistently approach self-care from a balanced, mindful, and compassionate perspective. These practices enable you to be successful and enjoy your life, family, and work. A quote that always comes to mind for me (by Dolly Parton) is "Don't be so busy making a living that you forget to make a life." The four pillars support you in actualizing the healthiest and happiest version of yourself and your life.

When clients come to us for their first wellness advisory consultation, we want to understand where the four pillars show up in their lives. We can determine the ingredients they already have in place and figure out the complementary ingredients to create balance and help them thrive. When we are in our lives, it can be hard to see the forest through the trees. We have blind spots, and sometimes small shifts can make a huge difference. For example, I met with a new client who was going to spin class six days a week but had no strength training. She felt weak and tired despite a rigorous fitness routine. We replaced two of her spin classes with personal training and yoga and added bodywork sessions two times a month. She felt exponentially better.

Another gentleman runs and plays golf but has chronic knee and back pain. He came to us because he believed he needed consistent massage. A once-a-week massage will help, but it will only scratch the surface of his situation. If he plans to manage his pain or optimize his golf game, he'll need to integrate mindful stretching and breathing (i.e., yoga). But we meet our clients where they are, and sometimes we need to give them what they think they need, build trust, and then make suggestions about what we know, based on experience and research, to *really* move the needle on their situation. We find that as clients begin to feel better, they're more willing to explore and add other practices. Helping clients cultivate a mindful perspective and listen to their bodies, hearts, and minds from the inside out is a huge part of the process. Oftentimes people know the answers; they are just not listening well or need a framework like the four pillars to interpret the messages they may be getting from their bodies.

The practices within the pillars of movement, stillness, touch, and nourishment don't appear out of nowhere, nor do you reap the full benefit by working with only one. The integration of these life ingredients needs to be highly intentional and supported by teachers, coaches, therapists, and community in our fast-paced digital world. When you practice elements of each pillar, an intricate web of self-care begins to support and cradle you in a space that allows you to let go. You begin to realize the world won't fall apart if you wait twenty minutes to check your email. As a result, you start to feel like you are leading a healthier, happier life.

All that said, you have to begin somewhere. When you begin the journey with one of the pillars, your curiosity to experience the other pillars will grow. Deep down we all crave a healthy state of dynamic equilibrium, and as you begin to peel off the layers of resistance and become open to the potential of greater balance, you will look for practices to build on the ones you're already engaged in. When you start to feel well, you'll want to feel well more often, and you'll look for ways and practices to make that happen. You'll also notice that when you feel good in and about yourself, you see the best in other people. This is where the true magic begins to happen. But of course, it's not really magic because it's entirely real and achievable.

You can begin using the practices to reinforce one pillar at a time, but know that you'll see the most benefits when all four sustain you. In this book, I'll give you lots of options for the types of practices you can integrate from each of the pillars. That way, you can choose those that are most appealing to you. Just like baking a cake, some of us prefer chocolate, and others love vanilla. Engaging in practices that we genuinely feel drawn to makes the integration of the four pillars feel natural and authentic. It's about experiencing the best version of you, as opposed to trying to be someone you're not.

Over time in the ever-evolving stages of your life, the practices that resonate for you will change. Be kind to yourself and open to adopting what's feels right at any given time.

BEGIN YOUR JOURNEY

For over twenty years, I've worked with an elite, ultra-successful clientele, many of whom would be considered captains of industry and world-class in what they do. From the outside, these people seem to have it all—high-powered jobs, urban penthouses and weekend country homes, European vacations, nannies, housekeepers, and prep school through Ivy League education for their children. Yet, just like many of us, their lives are rushed, their physical or mental health may be suffering, and their relationships can be unfulfilling. While they have everything money can buy, like most of us, they yearn for what I call "inner wealth."

Some of their problems may seem like first-world problems—and they are—but all the success in the world does not impact their susceptibility to the pain and suffering of the human condition. And sometimes their extreme success in certain areas of life exacerbates the tendency toward imbalance, overdoing it, and underdoing it. Before beginning my wellness business and teaching yoga and meditation full-time, I was a clinical social worker working with extremely disenfranchised individuals and families in inner-city neighborhoods. What struck me was that my social work clients with extremely limited resources faced very similar challenges to my ultra-successful wellness clients despite the fact that their lives were so different in many ways: worries about children and relationships, feeling rushed and overwhelmed, managing health and time, concerns about aging parents, substance abuse, and, of course, money. While, of course, my wellness clients had it exponentially easier in many ways, at the end of the day they seemed equally happy and equally as miserable as many of my social work clients. I felt as though I was beginning to understand the nature of the human experience.

The wisdom and knowledge I share in this book is extracted from my work with ultra-high performers but carries with it the wisdom of having worked with a wide range of human beings—old and young, rich and poor—throughout my career. These ideas can be implemented by anyone, anywhere, anytime. The four pillars mitigate the liabilities of our strengths, so we can still optimize and be the rock stars that we are. The four pillars shine light on our blind spots that cause us, and those around us, pain and suffering.

IT'S ABOUT THE JOURNEY, NOT THE DESTINATION

My husband and I take our three children on long, challenging hikes as often as possible. During the hike, when they start to look frustrated and whine that we'll never reach the top of the mountain, I tell them, "Look at the next big tree. Let's get to that tree." Each tree is a mini high five, and the hike is made up of passing one tree at a time and celebrating our progress. This reminds us that it's less about the ultimate destination, and more about reveling in our mini successes along the journey.

Oftentimes it's a crisis that causes us to stop in our tracks and figure out how to take care of ourselves, making a challenging situation a gift in some ways. That's said, my hope is that the stories in this book will serve as an impetus and inspiration to think about our relationship to self-care ahead of that breaking point. Self-care and personal growth are like hiking that challenging mountain. It's important to continually find new aspirations and honor our small wins. It's not about reaching one big goal and stopping there, but about being engaged in the process of our own development and evolution. We will encounter pain and obstacles inevitably, but every moment and milestone along the path has the potential to provide substance and learning, opportunity for strength and courage, and oftentimes a great deal of fun and joy.

THE ART OF LIVING

A mindful perspective makes space for the whole realm of experiences we will encounter without judgment, aversion, or grasping. The ability to be on the journey itself, as opposed to yearning for a past or future that doesn't yet exist, makes every moment and every day the most important one. It's not that we don't want goals to achieve, but feeling fully and finding joy in our work is essential. Because of our culture and education system, it's very easy to lose the plot and forget that our lives can be a work of art.

My nana Elaine had the following poem framed in her home, and now it is framed in my own home. I have found the message to be a very powerful reminder throughout my life.

Prayer for Now

Normal day, let me be aware of the treasure you are.

Let me learn from you, love you, bless you before you depart.

Let me not pass you by in quest of some rare and perfect tomorrow.

Let me hold you while I may, for it may not always be so.

—MARY JEAN IRION

I want to live in a way where a simple "normal day" is beautiful and enough. Life is short, and we're often so future-oriented that we miss the here and now. Life is not about being in search of some rare and perfect tomorrow. Life is about figuring out how to weave these ideas into our day-to-day to create a balanced existence, so our normal days feel precious and powerful.

This isn't an extraordinary feat or available only to the 1 percent. Yes, they have access to a tremendous amount of advice and support around self-care, but the truth is this precious normalcy is attainable by almost anyone living in the free world. In theory it's neither hard nor expensive, but it does take thought and dedication to care for your own self. The mindset I use with my clients is "start where you are." Where you are now is here. And here is beautiful.

Shall we begin?

THE FIRST PILLAR: MOVEMENT

An early-morning walk is a blessing for the whole day.

—HENRY DAVID THOREAU

Our bodies were built to move—our prehistoric ancestors moved all day long, hunting woolly mammoths and gathering edible berries. When we shifted to an agrarian society, movement was still part of most people's daily lives. In the last century or so, we've become more and more sedentary, and our modern health problems, mental and physical, reflect our lifestyle.

Movement helps us develop a sense of balance—again, both mental and physical. Research has proven that physical activity improves our brain function, acts as a natural antidepressant, and improves the aging process. Dr. Wendy Suzuki, a world-renowned neuroscientist (who I have had the pleasure of meeting), conducts research on brain plasticity. Her most recent work focuses on the impact of aerobic exercise on memory, learning, and cognition. Julia Basso and Wendy Suzuki explain in a review titled "The Effects of Acute Exercise on Mood, Cognition, Neurophysiology, and Neurochemical Pathways":

"Because of the role of exercise in enhancing neurogenesis

and brain plasticity, physical activity may serve as a potential therapeutic tool to prevent, delay, or treat cognitive decline. Indeed, studies in both rodents and humans have shown that long-term exercise is helpful in both delaying the onset of cognitive decline and dementia as well as improving symptoms in patients with an already existing diagnosis...Additionally, acute exercise has been shown to enhance affective, mood, and emotional states."[1]

In this first pillar, we explore three types of movement: programmed movement or scheduled fitness and exercise, integrated movement or those movements that we can do throughout the day, and yoga, which involves stretching and breathing.

Remember, it's not movement alone or a specific movement modality that will transform us. It's movement in conjunction with evidence-based fitness and wellness practices from the other three pillars that ultimately moves the needle on the gauge to inner wealth.

---

1   Julia C. Basso, Wendy A. Suzuki. "The Effects of Acute Exercise on Mood, Cognition, Neurophysiology, and Neurochemical Pathways: A Review." *Brain Plasticity*, 2017; 2(2): 127–152.

Chapter One

GET MOVING

Michael Copeland was hunched low like a lion waiting for the optimum moment to pounce on a gazelle. Then he pounced, swiftly and gracefully, and returned to the previous pose. At fifty-five, he moved through these physical postures with the same strength and ease as he moved through his life.

Michael knows his only competition is himself, and he came to Namaste to up his game. A captain of industry in real estate, he played golf and tennis with colleagues, ran marathons and triathlons, but could feel that he wasn't physically as spry as he'd been in previous years. He knew that if he didn't maintain his strength and flexibility along with his myriad of athletic interests, he wouldn't be able to dominate his sports in a way that fed his competitive nature. Michael's only requirements were that we make it fun and that he could measure results.

We began with twice-a-week sessions with a personal trainer but quickly learned that his weakness was not a lack of strength as much as a lack of flexibility, mobility, and embodiment. Yoga would be perfect for him, but he thought yoga was boring. The trainer met Michael where he was and captivated him with animal-based movement. These three-dimensional movements work the body in a circular, holistic fashion, and helped Michael get in touch with his body and build strength and mobility in a new and playful way—that took care of the fun part. Michael also wanted to measure his progress because he is results-driven. How, though, are wildebeest movements measured?

We worked with him to write down how he felt in certain physical forms. Rather than measuring how many reps he could do or how much weight he could bench-press, we asked him to assign a number to the tension he felt in his low back. The beauty of these metrics is that they come from the inside out, not from the outside in. Week after week, as he built deeper core strength and mobility, the tension level and associated number dropped. This progress gave him the competitive edge he sought for his other sports and activities.

When Michael first came to us, he thought he needed strength training. It was hard for him to let the trainer guide him as he is a brilliant man, used to knowing the answers. Yet he was smart enough to know that some-times it's important to take the seat of the student, and he trusted Namaste. When he saw the improvements in his other endeavors—like more fluidity and balance in his golf game and less pain during running—he shifted to a place where he was fully willing to surrender con-trol and immerse himself in the learning experience with his trainer.

A lot of high achievers have a hard time ever being fin-ished. They want to keep mastering new activities and developing themselves in different ways. Michael is one of those people, using sports and fitness as a way to con-tinue to achieve. Once trust was established with the trainer, he was able to reframe his goals and intentions and open himself up to a more interesting, enjoyable experience. He got the outcome he was looking for in terms of improving his performance and feeling better in his body. More than that, though, he also learned to be comfortable in the not knowing; he discovered that being receptive and practicing the art of learning was equally if not more valuable to him than winning a great race.

In other words, Michael embraced a beginner's mind—a beautiful place where a lot of potential lies. Beginner's mind is about seeing the world with fresh eyes and letting go of preconceived ideas and rules. A beginner's mind is empty. High achievers are often too smart for their own good and end up missing the opportunity that lies in not knowing. Educated, experienced, and at the top of their profession, high achievers may think they have all the answers, which limits potential for continued evolution. Beginner's mind invites curiosity and deep listening, which are key to innovation and solving complex problems. Becoming aware of our cognitive biases and judgmental inner dialogue is an important part of the process and is cultivated most directly by a mindfulness practice that we will discuss later in this book. When we can hold the fear of not knowing at bay, life opens up and keeps us engaged (and ready to pounce).

PROGRAMMED MOVEMENT AKA WORKING OUT

Amy Cunningham was getting married in nine months. On paper, Amy looked great: At thirty-two, she'd graduated with honors from Harvard Law School, was an up-and-coming partner at one of the more prominent firms on the East Coast, played golf with her peers, went on a yearly ski week vacation, and spent summer weekends in the Hamptons. In person, however, Amy was overweight, out of shape, and dealing with the back pain that comes from sitting at a computer and poring over legal briefs all day. She wanted to look and feel beautiful physically and mentally for her wedding day, and cultivate a healthier version of herself for the next chapter of her life.

Given Amy's schedule, she began doing private yoga and interval training in the early mornings. Her personal trainer, who is cross-trained as a yoga teacher and Pilates mat instructor, implemented a combination of cardio for lung and heart health, bodyweight exercises, TRX and BOSU ball fun, therapeutic Pilates mat work, and yoga geared toward back health and stress reduction. During and after her sessions, Amy was reminded of how she felt when she ran track in high school. She would practice with the track team after school, then come home and do her homework, her mind sharp from the endorphins and adrenaline released by the physical activity. The same thing happened when she added movement to her morning routine: she got to the office with a crisp and focused headspace, full of energy to face the day's tasks.

The trainer integrated brief guided meditations at the end of Amy's sessions, too. She was coming up on a big life event that required reflection and intention setting. Meditation helped her develop an awareness of the significance of her upcoming wedding day and the changes that event would bring to her life. She tuned in to what she was excited about and what she was petrified of, enabling her to be less reactionary when these feelings bubbled up. Our intention was to help Amy look and feel great on her wedding day from the inside out, and set her up for continuity with these practices post-wedding. The next phase of her life would mean juggling work and family, and perhaps becoming a mother. While it was Amy's wedding that spurred her to start thinking about her wellness, she was smart enough to know that she wanted to enter this chapter optimized.

I've known Amy and her mother for a long time, and they both told me that Amy's investment in these sessions pre-wedding was the most essential part of the preparation for what was an extravagant and expensive wedding. She was transformed on many levels, and in a position to enter marriage with mindfulness, strength, and a feeling of confidence and balance. She lost the extra pounds, and her back pain subsided. What's more, because of her balanced approach, Amy felt like her best self, without pressure to be perfect. The words Amy herself used to describe her pre-wedding state in light of her self-care routine was "centered, open, and strong."

HEALTHY HABITS

Amy's story is not uncommon, and it underscores a key point: it doesn't matter what gets us moving as long as we get moving. A major life event is a fantastic inspiration. The hardest part is starting, but once we begin to feel the benefits of the practice of movement or self-care in general, it tends to propel itself forward naturally. We all have our own reasons for exercise. Some people are interested in weight loss, competition, strength, longevity, or general health, while others—like me—know that exercise will help my mind and mood and help me manage stress and focus on my priorities throughout the day. Once our new patterns are ingrained in our life, we don't want to let them go.

Keep in mind that our wellness needs will constantly evolve based on the stages of our life. When we're in college, our life is focused on studying and friends. When we begin to work or start a family, our priorities shift. And then again as we age or retire, our intentions evolve further. What we need when we are healthy is sometimes very different than what we need when we are battling acute or chronic illness or going through a challenging time.

Programmed fitness is an essential part of wellness, but the reality is there are days when we may not have time for a full workout, such as when we are traveling or have a sick child at home. We can, however, weave practices throughout our day to respect the body and mind's need for movement. My husband coined the phrase "random acts of yoga," for example, to refer to those moments when we drop into a forward bend while the coffee brews or we're waiting for our luggage at the airport. I like to do shoulder rolls whenever I wait in line. We've all heard hacks such as "take the stairs, not the elevator" or "park farther away and walk." Let's look at how we can integrate meaningful movement throughout our day.

INTEGRATED MOVEMENT

A client of mine works in a large financial institution with a beautiful and spacious office. Instead of sending an email or instant message to a colleague, she walks to the other side of the office to her colleague's desk and asks her question. Not only is it a way to build movement breaks into her day, but she also reports that it is part of the secret to her professional success. She has small conversations all day long that enable her to connect with her colleagues in a deeper way that email or instant messaging doesn't allow.

Another extremely successful client who has built and sold several technology companies schedules "walk and talk" meetings with colleagues in the park whenever possible. He finds that this generates better ideas, builds relationships, and checks the movement box in a meaningful way. When asked how he takes notes during those meetings, he answered that anything really good or important will be remembered, and he leaves a ten-minute window when he returns to his desk to jot down key takeaways and next steps. He believes the practice and associated tools such as "the memory palace" that he uses to remember key ideas is great exercise for his mind, and he is right. The memory palace technique involves associating an idea to something very familiar such as a room in your home or your childhood bedroom, which enables you to place the ideas in locations you already have strong memories of.[2] And of course, walking in and of itself improves our memory, so one might argue that it's better to walk and think than to sit and think.[3]

I suggest clients look at their energy levels and patterns throughout the day to identify moments when integrative or mini movement practices would support their bodies and minds. For example, if we have trouble winding down at the end of the day to sleep, do a few forward bends, which are calming. Even five to ten push-ups every morning before hopping into the shower can provide a moment of exercise when the day is too busy for a full hour-long session with a trainer. My favorite of all is the coffee brewing dance time, as this discussion on movement would not be complete without mentioning one of the most powerful, primal movement expressions available—dance. Dance is therapeutic to body and mind, helping us integrate our emotional, physical, cognitive, and social experiences. Dance has the capacity to cultivate joy and self-esteem, and release built-up tension in the mind and body. Whether we dance to our favorite tunes organically and intuitively for five minutes in our kitchen while the coffee is brewing, go out dancing with

2   Ayisha Qureshi, Farwa Rizvi, Anjum Syed, Aqueel Shahid, Hana Manzoor. "The method of loci as a mnemonic device to facilitate learning in endocrinology leads to improvement in student performance as measured by assessments." *Advances in Physiology Education*, June 2014; 38(2): 140–144. https://www.ncbi.nlm.nih.gov/pmc/articles/PMC4056179/

3   Gretchen Reynolds. "Even a 10-Minute Walk May Be Good for the Brain." *New York Times*, October 24, 2018. https://www.nytimes.com/2018/10/24/well/move/exercise-brain-memory-fitness-cognitive.html

friends, or throw family dance parties with our children, those same feel-good endorphins that happen when we run also happen when we move our hips, arms, and feet and jump around the kitchen table. Music combined with movement, even for just a few minutes, is one of the most powerful, primal, and ancient stress relievers available to human beings.

So many of us spend an enormous amount of time sitting, and even that hour in the gym—if we get it—doesn't provide enough of the movement our bodies and minds need throughout a given day. Studies have shown that students have better attention and learning with integrative movement breaks. This applies to all of us, from young children to college-age kids to adults of all ages.[4] That said, we may have the best intentions but then look at the clock and realize we haven't moved our eyes from the screen for three and a half hours. Setting a timer that rings every sixty or ninety minutes is a great way to remember to stretch, breathe, take a walk to the water cooler or around the block, say an affirmation, or touch our toes. Taking one deep inhale and exhale is the perfect place to begin for people who think taking a break is too difficult. Is that too much to ask of ourselves? The goal is to weave self-care throughout the day. Day to day,

4   Barbara Fenesi, Kristen Lucibello, Joseph A. Kim, Jennifer J. Heisz. "Sweat So You Don't Forget: Exercise Breaks During a University Lecture Increase On-Task Attention and Learning." *Journal of Applied Research in Memory and Cognition*, June 2018; 7(2): 261-269. https://www.sciencedirect.com/science/article/pii/S2211368116301929?via%3Dihub

moment to moment, getting our heart rate up and our blood flowing will enable us to think better, work better, and engage more actively with our colleagues, friends, and family. And as natural law teaches us, that which goes up must come down. Integrative movements to calm our nervous system and tune us in to our bodies in a quieter way will enable us to listen, ground, and feel more peaceful.

Disconnection and disembodiment happen because we're hyper-connected to everything outside of us via the digital world, and we're "on" 24/7. Mental, emotional, and physical deterioration can creep up and manifest without us even realizing it. We're sitting at our desks for ten years, barely moving, never breathing deeply, never stretching—and then we wonder why we've got back pain and don't sleep well. Going to the gym three times a week doesn't begin to counterbalance what's happening the other 165 hours in the week. Even seven hours of self-care a week barely puts a dent in the pattern that develops throughout a lifetime of sedentary, stressful work. As much as the larger chunks of time are important for progressing, building strength, creating mobility, and doing deeper work, the integrated movements throughout the day are what bolster us against modern-day lifestyles and the influence of the digital world.

MOVEMENT CHANGES OUR LIFE

Noel Peterson still goes to his office at a prestigious Bay Area university where he has been a world-renowned medical researcher for forty years. He has achieved greatness in his career and takes pride in what he has accomplished. He's in his late seventies and recently has fallen a few times. While he's played doubles tennis sporadically throughout his life, he's never gone to the gym or worked with a trainer. Although a neurologist had ruled out any serious causes, the falls concerned Noel, and he thought he should do something to work on his balance and strength. He asked us for help, and we started by sending him a personal trainer.

Noel was set in his ways and wasn't willing to change his schedule too much. He got up early each day, had breakfast with his wife, read the newspaper, and then went to the office. He agreed to get up a half hour earlier three days a week to work with the trainer, and to do short, trainer-prescribed ten-minute routines on the other days.

His mini practices consisted of squats, push-ups with his knees on the ground, forward bends while holding onto the kitchen counter, leg lifts, and assisted (feet under the couch) crunches. His trainer encouraged him to do shoulder rolls, neck rolls, and ankle rolls during the day at his desk to help him stretch and become limber, as well as seated leg lifts. His trainer also encouraged him to take a daily walk at lunchtime for cardiovascular strength, and to practice applying the balance and awareness work that were the initial intention of his decision to engage in training.

Noel is a cerebral man, having spent a lifetime in his head. The trainer we sent is a salt-of-the-earth type of woman, completely embodied, street smart, and pragmatic. Noel was intrigued by her energy and attitude. He approached life from his head, and she approached life from her heart and her gut. He enjoyed spending time with her.

His decision to work with a trainer was a rational one. The doctors couldn't find anything wrong with him and chalked his falls up to aging. His wife, who is younger than he is, pushed him to do something because she wanted to avoid a situation where he took a fall and ended up in the hospital. She wanted an active companion and the best for him. Noel was a good student, diligent about doing the routine, and quickly began to feel stronger. After just a few months, he said he was moving better than he had since he was a young man. Noel's colleagues noticed that he was more animated, open, and engaged in their work. He told them about the personal experiences he was having with fitness, and how he felt like a younger version of himself. Feeling strong and connected in his body seemed to dramatically impact his sense of self-competency as he aged. Noel was excited about taking control over the next chapter of his life, although he hadn't given it much thought until he began declining. Changing his routine enabled him to experience a side of himself that he didn't know existed.

Throughout my years of working with people, I have seen firsthand that we have to have a strong ego (not to be confused with a big ego) in order to let go of our ego. Likewise, we need consistent patterns in our life to ground and anchor us, but if we become stuck creatures of habit, we miss out on a lot of potential. While certain habits can be very positive, continuing to learn and grow as older adults is one of the keys to longevity. Working with a great personal trainer is a powerful tool to continue to evolve through the years. Not only can a trained fitness professional help us avoid injury, but this type of a relationship with any degree of consistency, from a few times a week to once or twice a month, also keeps us on the fitness wagon and accountable to our goals and intentions. Simply investing money and time in our physical wellbeing helps us prioritize it in our life. A personal trainer can also enable us to intelligently change our routine to keep our bodies and minds growing and expanding without getting stuck in a repetitive rut, which is ultimately uninspiring and, even in the case of a consistent and rigorous routine, not necessarily a recipe for optimization.

It's never too late to take control of our health and well-being. Self-care is available in every chapter of our lives. Most of us want to build on positive, consistent habits rather than allow our habits to limit our ability to expand and grow. There's value in routine, but there's liability and risk of stagnation, too. Variety and saving space for new things goes hand in hand with consistency. Those statements can seem contradictory, but as with all aspects of self-care, the goal is balance.

Consistent rhythms are positive, but our needs change. Routines are great, but we have to listen to our bodies. We must know when it's time to shift gears in order to be in alignment with where we are in our life at that moment. If we wake up at 5 a.m. every day, maybe sometimes we need to sleep in. Running five miles every day is a great habit, but sometimes we need a rest—and the physical changes that happen as a natural course of aging are real. The goal is to build the habit of programmed and integrated movement but stay open to correcting course. Recognize when a habit isn't working anymore.

While programmed and integrated movement build and sustain our muscles, yoga takes a more holistic approach to movement, incorporating breath, mindfulness, and heartfulness. Yoga is a deep practice and can mean different things to different people. In the next chapter, we consider the heart of my practice.

Chapter Two

YOGA

Jonathan knew something was wrong the moment the pain in his hips and knees was so great that he had to cut his daily run short, something completely out of character for him as a type A entrepreneur. He began taking ibuprofen for the pain, a couple hundred milligrams in the morning, another pill or two in the evening. The pills allowed him to keep up his workouts and push through. Then one day, something clicked. He thought of himself as a young man—he was in his early forties—yet the pain in his hips and knees made him resistant to sitting on the floor to play with his children. He found himself sitting on the sofa and literally talking down to them. *What am I doing?* he thought to himself. *I've got chronic pain and I am popping pills all day to get relief.* Something had to change.

When Jonathan first came to Namaste, we traced the changes in his fitness routine back to five years prior when he became a father. By the time he had three children, the free time he used to fill with reading, visiting museums, and learning new things was now filled with being a dad. He loved being a father, and at the same time, he was concerned that he wasn't balancing time for his family with some time for himself. His intentions were in the right place; his application, however, led to a perfect storm of chronic pain and imbalance. He'd structured his self-guided routine around intensive workouts: low-rep, high-weight training in the gym in the morning, followed by a ten-mile run on the treadmill while watching the news. When we first met, his hamstrings were on lockdown and intensely tight, creating tension that rose through his hips, into his lower back, and up through his shoulders and neck. His body was so rigid that he could barely turn his head.

Albeit intense and high-performing, Jonathan is a glass-half-full, generally happy kind of man. He was eager to learn how to remedy his situation. When Jonathan and I had our first wellness advisory call, I learned about how he watched the news while running on the treadmill. While this was entertaining on a certain level, the content he was consuming often triggered feelings of stress. I explained that the tension that rose in his body while watching negative stories on the news caused physical stress and tightening of the muscles that was counterproductive to the benefits of running. And as we know, running in and of itself causes our muscles to tighten, even without the mental stress. I suggested he run outside instead—he lived next door to Central Park, where an urban lung waited to offer an experience of fresh, open air. He resisted a bit and agreed to run outside three days a week. He was shocked at how mentally invigorating this was to him compared to his treadmill and TV time—two totally different exercise experiences.

The real change for Jonathan came through adding a yoga practice to his evening routine. His children ate dinner around 6:30 in the evening and were in bed by 7:30. He got home early enough to spend a few minutes with them while they ate, tuck them in, and then eat dinner with his wife around eight. Their routine when we first met was to eat a heavy, late meal. I suggested they eat their big meal at lunchtime and then eat a light dinner. I then incorporated restorative evening yoga that focused on softening his tense, hardened muscles and led to a closing meditation practice.

Jonathan embraced yoga. He had always enjoyed learning new things, and he liked learning the alignment nuances of the poses, challenging himself with arm balances such as handstands and balancing poses such as standing on one leg, and the relaxation aspect that his teacher always incorporated into the wind-down and closing of the practice. He discovered the balance, new learning, and inspiration that he sought. Over time, Jonathan learned to use yoga positions to stretch and limber his muscles before his morning weightlifting and running routine, and he was able to eliminate the pain and the ibuprofen.

Yoga is a qualified physical exercise as well as a deep psychospiritual practice integrating aspects of both psychology and spirituality. Through the breathing, stretching, and mindful embodiment of yoga, we catch patterns and issues in our body, heart, and mind early on, before they blossom into full-blown injuries or problems. People who run, like Jonathan, are often extremely passionate—runner's high is a real thing. Their endorphins soar when they're running, and they often feel depressed when they stop. But they also tend to push themselves beyond the point that they should be running—something for which yoga provides a counterbalance.

The practice of yoga ripples off the mat and seeps into other activities as mindful awareness and a more embodied experience. Through yoga, Jonathan learned to be more present and compassionate in his body, understanding when he needed to slow down a bit and when he could push a little more.

As Jonathan worked with Namaste over time, we also added bodywork (which you'll read about in chapter nine), which supported his musculoskeletal system, his central nervous system, and his parasympathetic nervous system, all helping him to slow down and manage his stress. By integrating yoga and bodywork into Jonathan's self-care routine, he was not only able to continue running without pain or injury, but he was also able to release his stress physically and mentally and enjoy sitting on the floor with his young children, present, happy, and pain-free.

THE HEALING POWER OF YOGA

Eliza Stone didn't know how she'd feel from one morning to the next. She moved through her day-to-day routine but just didn't feel well. Eliza was diagnosed with an autoimmune disease several years ago, and she fought daily fatigue, aches, and chronic intestinal issues. Some days were better than others, but the unpredictable nature of her health kept her from going to her beloved spinning, barre, and yoga classes. Despite her doctor saying exercise wasn't the cause of her pain, the fitness classes seemed to exacerbate her symptoms and in turn create stress.

Eliza attempted to balance mothering two teenage children and holding leadership positions on several pres-tigious boards. She felt frustrated with her instability and how it impacted her capacity to feel effective as a leader and make meaningful contributions to the things she cared about. For years she tried to narrow down which foods or specific movements triggered her inflammation and pain. She often found herself wondering if something she ate yesterday had brought on pain. Or maybe it was something she ate last week? *It's a process*, she thought—a process she hadn't yet figured out.

Eliza lived in this constant wave of anxiety and uncertainty. What *was* certain, however, was that in addition to feeling mentally incompetent, she lacked the physical confidence she once had. She used to be incredibly active. She and her husband skied in Vermont every winter and hiked in the summer. Chronic back and knee pain, though, had made those outings impossible. She felt frustrated and vulnerable because her husband continued to be active and athletic, yet they could no longer do things together as they once did. She worried that she was disappointing her husband and that their relationship would suffer. Although I'm sure it was a loss for him, I'm also quite sure he had primarily compassion without blame for her.

Eliza came to us for a specific approach that kept her limitations in mind: she wanted to build muscular strength, navigate her pain, and reach her dream of hiking a substantial portion of the Long Trail with her husband for her fiftieth birthday, which was in a year.

We began with a restorative yoga practice. She was familiar with yoga and loved it, but she felt she was terrible at it. We reassured her that there's no such thing as a bad yoga practitioner. She looked fine from the outside, but inside she felt insecure, as if she was never doing a good job, and she was fearful of hurting herself. We created a modified practice that felt supportive and stabilizing to her neck and back and built strength in the musculature behind the kneecap. In a short amount of time, she made progress and began to feel stronger. We were able to integrate some personal training into Eliza's routine with a skilled and senior trainer adept at working with pain and injury, with the goal of building her cardiovascular stamina slowly and steadily.

Eliza did yoga twice a week and worked with a personal trainer once a week in between. She still dealt with all the symptoms of her autoimmune disease, but she felt physically and mentally stronger simply because she faced her situation head on, and she began to see small, incremental progress. By being proactive, she felt more in control of an out-of-control experience. This built confidence and a greater sense of connection with her husband, who occasionally joined her for her yoga and training sessions and practiced at Eliza's pace. After eleven months of her routine, Eliza was able to do an eight-hour hike on the Long Trail in Vermont with her husband just before she turned fifty. She never imagined being able to do this when she began with Namaste and felt a renewed sense of hope that at some point she would again put on skis and feel the energy of the slopes and the crisp mountain air, something she'd loved since childhood. Not surprisingly, as Eliza's physical confidence, stamina, and resilience grew, she felt more confident about her ability to lead as chairperson of the board and contribute meaningfully to the causes that mattered to her. It's not that her pain was gone, but her relationship to her body had changed dramatically, shifting her relationship to the rest of her life.

Yoga is an amazing practice because it always meets us where we are. We can do gentler poses on days we don't feel well and more rigorous and challenging poses on days we feel strong. Some days it makes sense to push ourselves, and other days surrender is the best choice. Yoga teaches us self-compassion and awareness, essential for embodiment and making wise decisions day by day, moment by moment.

Life is always going to present obstacles, and as Buddhist philosophy points out and my experiences have shown me, pain is an inevitable part of the human experience. Suffering, on the other hand, is a choice. There are things in life we can control and others we can't—like being diagnosed with an extremely challenging chronic disease. The work is to harness the things we do have control over, like our choices around movement and building strength of body and mind, in a way that can manifest certain ripples in our lives. As my own father always says, "It's not about the weight of the pack on your back but the strength of the back that carries the pack."

Eliza could have sat around and held a pity party for herself and suffered with her pain. Instead, she navigated the pain and grief by accessing her internal resources to build physical and mental strength, resiliency, and the ability to listen and find softness when she needed it most.

YOGA AND SELF-CARE

Yoga is the practice of being in our own skin. It is a loving mirror that shows us where we are physically and mentally, day by day, in our practice. Yoga can be moving meditation; the poses quickly bring us into our bodies consciously and hopefully compassionately. With practice we can observe where we feel tight and where we feel open and spacious, physically, mentally, and energetically. Combining movement and breathwork, we learn to be present in our bodies, and we notice when we are distracted by anxious thoughts or feelings without judgment.

Yoga is a feedback loop that touches on the four pillars simultaneously. Clearly it's movement, the meditative aspect falls into stillness, it nourishes the mind and body, and it offers touch and connection to ourselves and/or to the teacher. Yoga is one of the few physical practices where we literally wrap our arms around our bodies, essentially giving ourselves hugs.

According to yogic philosophy, the body has seven energy centers, or chakras, distributed from the tailbone to just above the crown of the head. Different types of energy flow—or can be blocked—at each of these centers. The asanas, or poses, stimulate the chakras, moving energy from one to another and to the meridians that are like a web, reaching the extremes of the body.

The asanas create balance. Different poses support opening (like backbends) and looking inward (forward bends). Exhalation and inhalation of the breath signal giving and receiving, connecting us to a universal pool of air that everyone on the earth is sharing.

A consistent yoga practice brings the body and all the internal organs into a greater state of harmony. Many people in their seventies and eighties who have practiced yoga throughout their adult life move with a fluidity rarely seen at that age. I had a wonderful, impeccable, and very fancy senior who I taught from age seventy to eighty. Her goal was to do a headstand, and by the time she reached her seventy-seventh birthday, she accomplished this magnificent feat. While I was a bit nervous, she was determined and empowered by the process and the achievement. My partner and husband, Michael, calls yoga the fountain of youth, and he is right. Yoga creates a quality of strength and mobility in body, mind, and spirit that are the essential, necessary ingredients for a balanced, rich, beautifully layered self-care practice.

IT'S OKAY TO CRY

Tears seeped from Alex McLaughlin's eyes with each exhale shortly after she sat on her yoga mat. She often cried spontaneously during the private sessions with her yoga teacher. It was the one time she could let her guard down, be vulnerable, and release the tension she wore like a coat of armor.

Alex was going through a personal crisis that had been years in the making. In her early twenties, she married the man she loved, but over time he had become abusive, unpredictable, and mentally unstable. She never knew when she woke up if he'd slam the door or bring her coffee in bed. She put up with the abuse because when he was nice, he was truly loving. And they had three children together. The pain was constant, but the crisis hit when she discovered he'd been unfaithful.

Alex did what so many of us do: she controlled the pain by creating an illusion of the perfect life. She was a wildly successful and renowned interior designer; the latest haute couture hung in her closet; her hair, makeup, and nails were always fresh from the salon. Her three children were perfectly dressed and mannered as well. She invested in protecting them and being a supermom. She followed an intense daily fitness and yoga practice, resulting in a sculpted body that was as beautiful and as hard as the statue of Venus.

Alex was physically strong but rigid. She knew she needed the softness of yoga. She knew she needed to feel. When she stepped on the mat, she was able to begin processing the emotional trauma she felt in her body. The yoga mat was the one place she could breathe, stretch, open, and release the feelings that she held tightly inside her rock-hard body.

Perhaps unconsciously, she thought that if she had the perfect body, the perfect children, and the perfect lifestyle, her husband would be faithful and kind again. She took him to therapists and interventions to try to "fix" him, hoping that he'd have an awakening and her family could be happy. At some level, they loved each other. He went to therapy because of her, not because he wanted to heal.

As Alex allowed herself pockets of vulnerability and emotional safety on the yoga mat, she softened. She was able to connect to her own experience rather than remain codependent on everyone else in the situation.

Over the course of five or six years, through her practice and psychotherapy, she was able to leave the relationship. The moment she made the decision, she stopped feeling the need to exercise with such intensity. She was comfortable being more real and less perfect. Her strength was balanced with softness, which I found to be more beautiful than the "perfect body" she'd had before. She transformed into a brave, strong but supple, gorgeous human being.

Yoga allows us to experience our lives from the inside out, rather than from the outside in, and that transformation takes time. Sometimes we need the darkness to get to the light, we need to be sick in order to heal, we need too much of something to find balance. That's the nature of life. When we understand the impermanence of the stages we go through in life, we can engage in the effort and surrender it takes to find mind-body health. When we're active in the process, we're not stuck, which means we're growing and evolving, moving through pain and pleasure. That's the art of living.

The practice of self-care is steady, but what it looks like will shift and change as life evolves. The more we can be curious about the emotional, mental, and physical landscape in this work, the more we're inspired to be consistent with our self-care. It's not about "set it and forget it" but about "let me engage in this journey," which serves consistency in self-care, whatever that might mean in different stages of life. When we get stuck in a practice that doesn't serve us, we become disengaged and often stop practicing altogether. When we figure out the right practice at any given moment, it feels like the path of least resistance, like we are in the flow of our life, even though it still takes effort and intention.

I'M TOO INFLEXIBLE FOR YOGA

All the time, I hear people who say, "I'm too inflexible for yoga" or "yoga's boring." First of all, there is no such thing as being bad at yoga. Yoga is a practice, not a performance, so there's no reason we can't do it whether we're as limber as a contortionist or as stiff as a board. There is no winner—there is no loser.

I'll say, "Let's just stretch and breathe." And they're okay with that. People are often worried about performing and doing well, but stretching and breathing is just a practice. My secret's out now—I trick them into doing yoga, which is essentially stretching and breathing.

Just like there is no such thing as being bad at yoga, I am not overly impressed if someone can wrap her leg around her neck ten times. I am interested only in the quality of the breath, heart, and mind during the movements. Yoga is a lifelong practice, and progress happens over years. It's an investment in our health and well-being, and the return on investment comes with time.

The true intention of the practice is to work through tension in the body and mind and to prepare the body for meditation. Contrary to popular belief, one could argue that the tighter we are, the more yoga we should do. It's not about how flexible we are today; it's about learning to be in our own skin in the tension in our body, listening and breathing into that.

JUST BREATHE

By the time Stan Goodman's wife convinced him to call Namaste, he had been holding his breath for about forty years. He had a happy marriage, his children were in college, he was a top executive for a fashion conglomerate—life was good. His expression, however, was of someone in chronic pain, and his tight lips told me the guy barely breathed. Every muscle from his forehead to his toes was taut with the tension of stress, travel, sitting, and random, inefficient exercise. His shoulders were so close to his ears that it seemed he didn't have a neck. Stan also had a phone addiction and had developed a forward-leaning neck from constantly staring at his screen. I could see the foreshadowing of a kyphotic hunchback. He didn't have acute pain, but he was deeply uncomfortable in his body.

Stan traveled a lot for work and ate his meals in airports and hotels, and while he knew he needed a self-care plan, he had a hard time being consistent. After about a year of on-again, off-again sessions, he finally committed to weekend sessions—both Saturday and Sunday. Through the consistency of those weekend "stretching and breathing" sessions (dare I call it yoga), Stan started to feel better, giving him a taste of what was possible if he could practice more frequently.

One Monday morning on a flight to Los Angeles, he

noticed that he could turn his head to talk to the passenger next to him—something he hadn't been able to do six months earlier. He'd had a yoga session the evening before and had an aha moment. Stan realized that the yoga practice was helping and that he needed to do it more often.

He began time-blocking. He worked with his assistant to schedule out yoga sessions two weeks at a time. When he was traveling, he'd have a thirty-minute virtual session with his teacher from his hotel room. Similar to the level of intensity he remembered having when launching his career in his twenties and tasting some success, Stan became obsessed with practicing yoga and how it was changing his experience in his body. We also integrated Pilates to build his core strength. He stuck to a consistent three-times-a-week schedule and became completely engaged in the experience of learning. Stan also began doing bodywork a few times a month, which he shared with his wife. Leveraging the support of some recorded guided sessions made by his yoga teacher, he practiced deep breathing and mindfulness meditation on long flights. Stan incorporated random acts of yoga into his day. When waiting in the airport, he'd do a forward fold with his arms on his suitcase. On one of his business trips to Asia, he even stayed an extra week and went on a yoga and wellness retreat with his wife.

Stan's body went through a total transformation. His

face was no longer tense, his posture was erect, and his furrowed brow had softened. His shoulders were down and open. He told me his mindset shifted from numbness toward his job to finding gratification in his work. The compassion he learned toward himself spread outward as well; he became concerned about the working conditions in his company's factories in Asia. He'd never given it a moment's thought before practicing yoga. He became more conscious, and compassion became the filter through which he viewed the world. He was residing in his body and his heart, no longer a talking head. He was living his life, playing and enjoying the game rather than just being a piece on the board.

THE POWER OF YOGA

Any movement is better than no movement, but over time, traditional fitness can create physical tension, rigidity, and even injury. Yoga helps mitigate the tension of sport and other types of exercise. As we saw with Alex McLaughlin, yoga offers softness to a body hardened by too much fitness. And as we saw with Stan Goodman, it can do so much more.

Yoga helps us learn to live in our bodies. Every experience, every emotion we have, is stored in the body. When we don't move in a way that enables us to energetically process those experiences and emotions, the energy gets stuck. On an emotional, psychological, and psychospiritual level, with the support of a skillful and highly trained teacher, the practice is a vehicle to process experiences and trauma that we hold in our bodies.

Yoga builds strength that is proportionate to our body (because we're not using weights); we're holding our own body in space. That kind of strength creates an equilibrium and suppleness. We're less prone to injury and more fluid and expansive physically as well as mentally and emotionally. Practiced over a lifetime, yoga leaves us looking and feeling younger than the biological number on our driver's license. We're able to sit cross-legged on the floor to play with our grandchildren.

Originally created as a way to prepare the body for long, sitting meditation, yoga practice always ends with Savasana, which is a final rest. This most important part of the practice has several purposes. It enables us to digest and integrate the benefits of the practice on multiple levels and leaves us restored and energized even after a rigorous class. Savasana is "the other half" of the stretching, strengthening, and flowing. It's the stillness, the quiet, and the returning to the earth. The combination of the movement and the stillness of yoga helps us live with greater ease in our bodies and teaches us how to be in our own skin in many different shapes and forms, literally and metaphorically. As important as it is to move and do, it is equally essential to stop and rest. Ironically, for many high-achieving people, it is the slowing down and the stillness that is the hardest. They have been trained to move and achieve and have been rewarded financially and otherwise for these accomplishments. Slowing down can be frightening. Facing the resistance to stillness, moving through the uncomfortable feeling of being in our own selves, and making space for doing less is key to inner wealth. This leads us to our next pillar: stillness.

THE FIRST PILLAR: MOVEMENT

QUESTIONS TO CONSIDER

- If you have physical pain, can you assign a number to it? Are there moments when the number is lower or higher? Are you aware of what makes the number or level of pain increase or decrease?
- Can you embrace a beginner's mind with regard to movement in your life? Are you willing to be a student and practice something new? Can you embrace a beginner's mind in other areas of your life such as work?
- Is there an event in your life that would inspire you to begin taking care of yourself?
- Could someone in your life be your accountability buddy, or is it time to get a personal trainer, teacher, or wellness coach?
- What fitness habits do you have that perhaps need to

change or evolve? Are you a creature of habit or stuck in your ways?

- When in your day can you add micro-movements, such as a forward bend or three push-ups? Could you imagine creating a habit of these micro-movements that's as consistent as brushing your teeth?
- Is your movement practice balanced? Could you benefit from restorative practices such as yoga, or do you need to pump it up with something more intense?
- Where have you created illusions of control in your life? Are you putting on a show to hide from the truth?

PRACTICES

- If your schedule is packed, and even if it's not, plugging movement sessions into your calendar in advance is a way to create accountability and consistency. Map out your workouts at least a week in advance. Make appointments with yourself and honor them as you would respect an appointment with a colleague or a friend.
- Don't fall down the digital rabbit hole. Set a timer on your computer while you are at work and take a movement break every hour. It can be as simple as going to the water cooler, or as intentional as practicing a few minutes of chair yoga at your desk.
- To energize, have fun, and manage anxiety, put on music and dance, even for five minutes while your

water boils or your coffee brews. Feel the music from the inside out and practice not caring what you look like; focus on how you feel.

- Strike a pose and do a random act of yoga. Roll your shoulders while you wait in line, do a few neck rolls while you make dinner, interlace your hands behind your back, and squeeze your shoulder blades together as you walk onto the tennis court or golf course.
- Deep breathing is one of the simplest, most restorative acts we can do. Try it right now—breathe in fully from your clavicle to the bottom of your belly, and breathe out, emptying the space from the bottom of your belly through the entire capacity of your lungs to your clavicle. Repeat anytime, anywhere.

THE SECOND PILLAR: STILLNESS

Guard well your spare moments. They are like uncut diamonds. Discard them and their value will never be known. Improve them and they will become the brightest gems in a useful life.

—RALPH WALDO EMERSON

No doubt movement is important, yet these days, people seem to keep driving forward without taking the time to rest. We live in an overstimulated, hyper-connected time. Society as a whole is struggling with this hyper-stimulant known as the digital connection, which also allows us to work all hours of the day and night. It's hard to unwind from that place.

Back in the day, before mobile phones and tablets, we spent time waiting. Those moments of waiting were an opportunity for stillness or connection. Before the digital onslaught, if we arrived early to a lunch appointment, we sat quietly and waited or, at most, read a book we'd brought until our date arrived. While waiting in line at the post office, we struck up a conversation with the person next to us or wrote our to-do list on the back of a receipt. Or maybe we simply enjoyed that we couldn't be anywhere else in that moment. For a while, airplanes were the last vestige of freedom from digital contact, and today, Wi-Fi connections are available even on transatlantic flights. Those natural, mindful moments that used to be part of the lives of regular people who don't live in an ashram—what I think of as "found moments"—are over. Even if we're not seeking enlightenment, we have to find moments of stillness just to stay sane. Otherwise, our entire life is one giant reaction to overstimulation.

We can be far healthier and more effective in our lives if we integrate restorative and relaxing moments consistently. Even moments of boredom where we need to learn how to be comfortable in our own skin are so vital. I tell my clients I want them to feel truly rested on a daily basis so that they don't *need* to take a vacation in order to unwind from their nonstop daily life. Wouldn't you like to feel that way, too? Meditation has been proven to reduce physiological markers of stress including cortisol, blood pressure, heart rate, and inflammatory markers. Mindfulness helps reduce the obsessive or fluctuating mind of people struggling with anxiety and improves attention.[5] Lack of sleep increases our risk of health problems, chronic disease, and even obesity.[6] Researchers have studied the practice of journaling and learned that this simple practice is beneficial for people struggling with eating disorders, mental illness, ADHD, and stress. In fact, successful people throughout history dating back to the tenth century in Japan, presidents, artists, and other famous people swear by the power of a simple writing practice.[7] The three parts of the Stillness Pillar—meditation, rest, and reflection—support a balanced, healthy life. Stillness provides the surrender to the strength of movement.[8] Stillness balances the doing with rest, recovery, reflection, and integration.

---

5 Mengran Xu, Christine Purdon, Paul Seli, Daniel Smilek. "Mindfulness and mind wandering: The protective effects of brief meditation in anxious individuals." *Consciousness and Cognition*, May 2017; 51: 157–165. https://www.sciencedirect.com/science/article/abs/pii/ S1053810016303142

6 Hassan S. Dashti, Frank A.J.L. Scheer, Paul F. Jacques, Stefania Lamon-Fava, José M. Ordovás. "Short Sleep Duration and Dietary Intake: Epidemiologic Evidence, Mechanisms, and Health Implications." *Advances in Nutrition*, November 2015; 6(6): 648–659. https://academic.oup. com/advances/article/6/6/648/4555142

7 Maud Purcell, LCSW, CEAP. "The Health Benefits of Journaling." *PsychCentral*, October 8, 2018. https://psychcentral.com/lib/the-health-benefits-of-journaling/

8 Michaela C. Pascoe, David R. Thompson, Zoe M. Jenkins, Chantal F. Ski. "Mindfulness mediates the physiological markers of stress: Systematic review and meta-analysis." *Journal of Psychiatric Research*, December 2017; 95: 156–178. https://www.sciencedirect.com/science/ article/abs/pii/S0022395617301462

Chapter Three

REST

As an entrepreneur, Joshua Gold struggled enormously with unplugging. His inbox had reached a level that put him instantly into fight-or-flight mode. He was so anxiety-ridden that meditation felt out of reach. We needed major scaffolding to support him in the process of teaching his nervous system how to relax. Many people who work hard in this digital day and age are struggling to regulate their nervous system, so Josh is not alone.

As his wellness advisor, the first time I spoke with Josh, we talked about creating an activity that would help him unplug. We also knew he needed to exercise and reside more in his body, in the moment. He lived by his calendar and time-blocked everything—if an activity was time-blocked, he did it. He went to his beach house on Long Island every weekend, and he agreed to time-block a one-hour, phone-free walk on the beach every Sunday as a starting point on the journey of finding balance. He could go alone or with his wife or a friend, but he couldn't take any devices with him.

Those Sunday walks became an anchor to his weekend and the only unplugged period of time in his week. To an outsider, a weekly walk on the beach seems like a simple, enjoyable, normal thing to do. For Josh, who had a lot of anxiety and whose phone was never more than two feet away, it was a big deal.

As summer came to a close, we had to recreate the experience in New York City. He agreed to a private session of yoga in his home each Saturday where he wasn't allowed to have his phone in the room. He began to see the benefits of having created this phone-free space in his life. On Sundays, he went for an hour-long walk in Central Park. The rules were the same as his weekly beach walk: his wife or a friend could join him, no devices. He required the support of his Namaste wellness coach to stay on the wagon when he experienced resistance to his tech-free commitment, and that was just what his coach was there for.

On his weekly walks, Josh not only had time to disconnect from his phone and live in his body, but because his wife often joined him, the time also became a point of connection for them as a couple and their relationship was nurtured, which was desperately needed. His wife had come to feel like a second priority to whatever was happening on his palm-sized screen. If his attention was any indication of his priorities, she felt low on the list.

After six months, the third thing we were able to incorporate into his life was a digital sunset during the weekdays. He was sleep-deprived because he was on his phone until midnight every evening. He agreed to turn his phone off and plug it in in the kitchen each evening at 10 p.m. No one needed to hear from him at that hour of the night, and I told him that sending email at that hour was "unbecoming." An article in the *New York Times* backed me up when they reported that unplugging is actually seen as a status symbol in their article "Human Contact Is Now a Luxury Good." Nighttime is best reserved for activities like reading, cuddling, lovemaking, or dining with friends.

With support from his wellness coach and a steady, intentional approach, Josh applied the discipline that helped him achieve financial success to unplugging, and the ripple effect was life-changing. As a result of the ping-pong effect of his anxiety and digital addiction, his work performance had been mediocre at best, his marriage had felt empty and disconnected, his body was unhealthy, and his mind was a stressed and scattered place. By making space for rest and reflection, he reconnected emotionally with people he loved, including himself.

He also began sleeping better, feeling inspired and creative at work, and overall experiencing the world from a healthier, happier place.

PENCILS DOWN

In today's society, we're working more hours than ever because we can. For many of us, every minute of our calendars is filled in with a work meeting or a social engagement. What little time we dedicate to relaxation is disguised as binge-watching Netflix or zoning out on Instagram. We're constantly absorbing information without taking the time to integrate it. When we live in the perpetual input-output mode of email, social media, and channels, we shut ourselves off from the world that lives within ourselves. Quite simply, we are doing too much. Rest is the partner to work. Undoing and reclaiming parts of ourselves lost to stress, trauma, and injury is essential in a world of productivity.

Young children have playtime, but as they grow up, we fill their playtime with sports practice, homework, and piano lessons. From early on, we buy into the message that life will pass us by if we're not doing something or bettering ourselves in some concrete way. Unlearning this message is key to our children's and our society's ability to thrive. When teaching a child, if the child isn't given the time to integrate what they've learned, their thinking is negatively affected, and true growth stagnates. Relaxation is the recovery time that is a natural part of integrating the work. It enables us to actually receive the teachings the world has to offer us.

At some point during the day, we need to say, "Pencils down." This is what the teachers used to say when I was a child in school, and the message was that even if we had one more sentence to write, time was up, and it was time to be done, even if we were not. Today, we will never be done. There is always another email to write, something we need to buy, or another post to read or like. The buzz needs to stop, devices and television off, calendar closed. We need the space to pause, to feel, and to breathe.

Pausing is uncomfortable for many, yet the dull ache of suffering that many people experience is a result of feeling like a stranger in our own bodies and minds, and not taking the time to visit our inner world. We don't like going into a place of nothingness because we have to face ourselves, so we fill our time with appointments, activities, and apps. But we're running on a treadmill that's a race to nowhere—day after day after day. When we cut out the stimulation, we're forced to sit in the space of our mind and body to both feel our pain and appreciate the joy in our lives. This is the heart of the experience of being alive.

Relaxation provides the space to integrate the different

aspects of our lives. It helps regulate our nervous system and sustains our relationships. Relaxation doesn't have to be luxurious, but it should be enjoyable. It can be as simple as lying in the grass to look at the clouds, cuddling on the couch, or taking a bath. It is these simple behaviors that help us mentally and physically process the experiences of our lives. When we take the time and make the space to discover ourselves, we can disengage from the grind and enter the mindset of greater trust and letting go. In turn, it's the device-free time that allows us to talk, listen, and connect with those around us.

We need to look for pockets of time during the course of the day for restorative moments. When we are wound up, we may need to fake it until we make it and take the actions needed to relax, before necessarily feeling inspired to relax. Putting actions before feelings can lead us to the feelings themselves—in this case, to the desire to drop into ourselves more deeply. For example, we might not feel like lying down with our kids for fifteen minutes, but after the first thirty seconds, we're giggling together or having an important conversation. Once we get over the initial anxiety about what might happen if we stop, if we don't answer that text message or send that email, if we miss the last episode of our favorite series, the calm has an opportunity to set in. When we drop out of our minds and into our bodies, a sigh of relief becomes more available. Our shoulders drop away from our ears, our facial muscles soften, and we can receive the moment we are in.

NOT A VACATION, NOT A DISTRACTION

For some, relaxing may be cooking a meal. For others, it might be a walk on the beach. Whatever relaxation we choose, it's not part of our daily grind, although it may be a hobby we practice each day. It's something that brings us joy and allows us to connect to ourselves.

Vacations and retreats are wonderful and important, but they don't replace the necessity of pausing for ten or fifteen minutes a day to unravel without external stimulation. It is those small moments that reinforce our nervous system and build resilience to the stressors of modern life.

Relaxation is also not scrolling through Instagram or Pinterest. I call those pleasurable distractions but not relaxation. It's important to understand that relaxation is also different than formal meditation. We practice meditation to bear witness to the patterns of our mind, focus, cultivate an intentional feeling, or just make space in our day. As I define it, relaxation has a pleasurable overtone to it and is meant to make space for drifting off into thoughts or fantasies, indulge our creativity, or dive deeply into our feelings.

LETTING GO

Our attachments can cause pain and suffering. We spend so much of our time attaining and maintaining our material possessions, our jobs, our appearance, our homes and cars, you name it—and the fear of losing any one of them can create feelings of deep anxiety. We're afraid that if we stop and let go for a moment, we'll lose all that we've worked for and identify with.

Relaxation is about letting go and trusting that we'll be okay if we just "be." It's about letting the journey of our lives flow through us and understanding that pleasure, freedom, and softness are meant to be a part of our experience of being alive.

I had a wellness advisory consultation with a woman who'd founded a successful startup in the wellness space. She told me about her robust self-care routines, which, despite being all great practices to engage in, left her feeling overscheduled and without a sense of spaciousness in her life. In the recommendations I sent to her after our consultation, I told her to do two fewer things. She needed more roominess in her life. Instead of going to yet another high-intensity fitness class, I suggested she take a relaxed and mindful walk in the park with a friend. We can apply this to our own life: Busyness is trending and has seeped into our work lives, our social lives, and even our self-care. While this book is about the ingredients for a delicious wellness recipe, more is not necessarily better. What can be removed from a busy schedule to create a little space for relaxation and discovery?

I love essential oils, for example, and I keep a few bottles and a diffuser on my nightstand, by my hot water pot where I make my morning tea, and in my home office. I also keep a few essential oil rollers in my pocketbook to have on the go. Each evening before I go to bed, I put a drop or two in my body lotion, massage my feet, and let the aromatic energy medicine infuse the air around me. I do another variation in the morning while I make my tea and take breaks in my workday to nurture myself with my chosen oils for focus and calm. Those mini moments dribbled through my day as nurturing touchpoints feel like they hold me in a daily embrace of self-care. Creating a sensory experience can be a powerful tool to drop into the moment, out of our minds and into our bodies, making for that relaxing pocket in a busy day.

These little reminders look different for everyone. Both my daughter and my son like to draw, and they leave their set of colored pencils and sketchbooks out. They can take a few minutes in the day to doodle or work on an illustration. Friends of mine love to play backgammon and leave a board out on their coffee table as a reminder so they are cued to pick up a game after school or on the weekend.

SLEEP

Our ability to execute on everything else depends on the quality of our sleep. For example, in speaking with a weight-loss client, who happens to be a senior executive at a major bank, she confessed that she scrolls through social media on her tablet for an hour or so before going to sleep as a way to "unwind." She suffers from insomnia and often wakes up tired, leaving her unmotivated to exercise or follow a healthy diet. She'll grab a caffeinated diet soda to boost her energy in the morning even though she knows it's detrimental to her well-being. We can have the best intentions to follow an exercise and nutrition plan, but sleep is a huge component of the success of any weight-loss plan or health goal. When we're well rested, our ability to manage cravings and stay on the fitness bandwagon improves. I know for myself that the day after I've had too little sleep, I tumble into all my pitfalls, using vices such as too much caffeine to get my body feeling right or media to manage my distracted mind. Of course, I am left feeling worse off, which can lead me to a cycle of less-than-optimal functioning.

Sleep begets sleep. Think of an overtired baby who can't sleep—adults are really no different. Yet we do so many things that are counterproductive to a restful night. We eat a late dinner or snack while watching late-night TV. We check email or social media one last time before turning out the lights, and what we thought would be a few minutes becomes forty-five—and that's forty-five fewer minutes of sleep. We then struggle to fall asleep because the backlit screens overstimulate our eyes and brains. Research published by the Salk Institute explains,

"For most, the time spent staring at screens—on computers, phones, iPads—constitutes many hours and can often disrupt sleep. Now, researchers have pinpointed how certain cells in the eye process ambient light and reset our internal clocks, the daily cycles of physiological processes known as the circadian rhythm. When these cells are exposed to artificial light late into the night, our internal clocks can get confused, resulting in a host of health issues."[9]

One of the best things I have done for my own sleep was to eliminate my phone from my bedroom. By doing so, I avoid that last-minute check, which helps me get seven hours of sleep instead of six. I've replaced the phone on my nightstand with a stack of books, calming essential oils as I mentioned, a journal, and a good old-fashioned alarm clock.

We tend to think of sleep in a vacuum, as opposed to understanding how it impacts all the other aspects of our lives in a profound way. What precedes sleep and happens

---

9   Salk Institute. "Why screen time can disrupt sleep: Scientists uncover how certain retinal cells respond to artificial illumination." *ScienceDaily*, November 27, 2019. https://www.sciencedaily. com/releases/2018/11/181127111044.htm

before bedtime impacts sleep quality, and everything that happens the next day is impacted by how well we slept the night before. It's an essential piece for our bodies and minds, like gas for a vehicle or a personal charging station. As Arianna Huffington said, "These two threads that run through our life—one pulling us into the world to achieve and make things happen, the other pulling us back from the world to nourish and replenish ourselves—can seem at odds, but in fact they reinforce each other."[10] We need to get in bed, close our eyes, and get charged to function optimally the next day.

Creating the invitation and space for relaxation can be the first step to making it a valuable part of our day. When we are well rested, we have the mental space and a more balanced nervous system to take the time for reflection, the second part of the second pillar. In addition to meditation and rest, stillness requires reflection, as we see in the next chapter.

---

10   Arianna Huffington. *The Sleep Revolution: Transforming Your Life, One Night at a Time.* Harmony Books (New York); reprint edition (April 4, 2017).

Chapter Four

REFLECTION

Skip Johnson excels at everything he does. A star athlete and extremely successful businessman, his intense type A personality certainly contributes to his success, but it also causes him mental and physical stress that impacts his sleep, the quality of his most intimate relationships, and his ability to feel happy and peaceful on a deeper level. He came to Namaste over a decade ago to figure out how to create pockets in his life to slow down, improve his sleep, and explore living with greater balance. An extremely bright and well-read person, he came to the table with a good deal of self-awareness about the patterns he wanted to change and was open to anything we suggested. He was what we call a "Zen CEO" in the making. We started with slow, mindful yoga and breathwork, which was a key balancing ingredient. With a Namaste teacher he respected deeply, he learned to meditate and used the space in sessions for existential conversation and contemplation.

The time Skip dedicated to yoga and meditation created reflective space that supported his sleep, his relationships, and his happiness and performance for the rest of his week. Fourteen years of practicing has enabled him to ride the wave of stressful stages in life and career with greater awareness and equilibrium. As an ultra-high performer, making space for non-doing was not familiar or necessarily natural to Skip. That practice—the not doing—had to be intentional, as it does for so many people today. Let's take a closer look.

THE SPACIOUSNESS OF NOT DOING

On a macro level, reflection is about slowing down and making space for feeling, noticing, and thinking. On a micro level, reflection shows up in practices like journaling, drawing or doodling, taking a walk with a friend, or stepping onto our yoga mat. For me, reflection often looks like taking five minutes away from my phone and computer and lying on the chaise lounge outside on a warm day to breathe, listen, and reflect.

Or when I approach a full inbox, reflection looks like pausing between responding to one email and the next. We spend so much time absorbing information from emails, texts, meetings, and videos without leaving space in between to process all the communications. Responding is a necessary part of our lives, but when I slow down and take a breath between each email to process, it changes the experience for myself as well as the quality of my interactions. After each email, I either let it go or file it in my mind or heart, and then read and consider what a thoughtful response to the next email would be. The practiced pause makes the process of getting through my inbox less stressful, even enjoyable and mindful.

The highest performers I know and have worked with value learning and continued growth in theory, although practice can be a challenge. Reflection is key to learning as a paper published by Harvard Business School explains. They propose that "one of the critical components of learning is reflection, or the intentional attempt to synthesize, abstract, and articulate the key lessons taught by experience." They found that the impact of reflection on learning is mediated by a perceived increased ability to achieve a goal, otherwise known as self-efficacy. They mention an important quote from the psychologist, philosopher, and educational reformer John Dewey: "We do not learn from experience...we learn from reflecting on experience."[11]

A moment of reflection can be as simple as a deep breath.

---

[11] Giada Di Stefano, Francesca Gino, Gary Pisano, Bradley R. Staats. "Making Experience Count: The Role of Reflection in Individual Learning." *Harvard Business School NOM Unit Working Paper No. 14-093; Harvard Business School Technology & Operations Mgt. Unit Working Paper No. 14-093; HEC Paris Research Paper No. SPE-2016-1181*, June 14, 2016. https://hbswk.hbs.edu/item/learning-by-thinking-how-reflection-improves-performance

It's a close cousin to mindfulness, and the lines between reflection, rest, and meditation are blurred—more of a soft, seeping charcoal line than a fine line. Reflection can also be as intense as working with a therapist and creating a compartmentalized space in our week to process feelings, thoughts, and worries in the context of a trusting relationship.

TAKING TIME TO THINK

Reflective time is thinking time, which leads to creative or innovative ideas and inspiration. Cal Newport, author of *Deep Work: Rules for Focused Success in a Distracted World*, explains in his book that removing distractions and working deeply, as well as embracing boredom by removing habitual, impulsive, and addictive tendencies like social media, are *key* to optimizing ourselves. Reflection is part of deep work, and it happens when we make space for our wisdom, insights, and ideas to surface and be heard by us.

Reflection is different than meditation, and as a component of deep work, it can be blocked for extended periods of time—several hours to whole days. Reflection can also happen more organically and have a softness about it—for example, my breath practice in between emails. Meditation comes with technique, whereas reflection is more open-ended, albeit intentional. Reflection can be looking out the window at the trees on a drive, having a quiet cup of tea at the end of a day, or calling on memories that cultivate a feeling of warmth and joy. Reflection can even feel like an indulgence, where we daydream or let our thoughts wander.

We talk so much about being in the present moment, and the word *reflection* can sound like thinking about the past or looking behind us. Reflection time can be filled with looking back, reminiscing, or visualizing plans for the future, but it is not meant to manifest ruminating or obsessive thoughts. Thinking back or ahead is important for learning from prior experiences and manifesting goals and intentions, but at the end of the day, we can only be here, now.

REFLECTION AND THE BODY

Francesca Horn was in her mid-forties when we met. She was a professional artist who sold her paintings for a small fortune, and she was on the board of a major New York City museum as well. Her husband, a renowned architect, had lost a long, difficult battle with cancer, and she was grieving. Her two children were preadolescents, and they were struggling deeply after watching their father die and experiencing the gaping hole that was left in his absence. Francesca had a huge amount of responsibility, and on top of sorting through her feelings, she had to sort out how to manage her life as a single mom and widow. She'd never practiced yoga or meditated in the formal sense of the word. Her art had always been her practice, but she now had no desire to paint. Her grief left her physically rigid and feeling far from the state of flow she experienced while she was being creative. Her body felt tight and cold from the inside out, and the world felt cruel and dark. As a single mom, she could not crawl under the covers and hide, although that was what she wanted to do. From the wisest place in herself, she knew that her only choice was to find a soft, warm, and nurturing space to grieve, breathe, and think about her changed life.

We started doing a full yoga practice with her three times a week—gentle asana, pranayama (breathwork), and meditation. Francesca found the most comfort in pranayama, and we created small practices that she could use throughout the day that allowed her to slow down and center her mind and heart. She practiced pranayama before waking her children for school, before picking them up, and then again before her own bedtime.

Francesca needed to make space for her grief. Giving her pain room to breathe, to express itself, and eventually to release was the key to her healing process. Pranayama allowed her to connect with and breathe out the pain, tension, grief, and emotions she was holding in her body, from her organs and muscles to deep in her bones. As she released the emotions, she was able to live with greater ease in her body and in her life overall. Francesca's anger at the world for the fact that she lost her husband, her frustration at having to raise her children alone, and her longing for intimacy with her soulmate were all living in the cells of her body. Reflection within the vehicle of slow, mindful movement created the dynamic therapeutic energy needed to permeate her grief-ridden rigidity and mobilize healing.

Reflection helps us release rigidity, because when we can think and feel, we have the opportunity to release blockages, enabling movement to happen.

CRAVING GRATITUDE

Reflection gives us time for gratitude, which is medicinal. A daily gratitude ritual improves long-term well-being by more than 10 percent.[12] [13] This incremental improvement is profound when you think of the simplicity of such a practice. The practice of gratitude creates a chemical shift in the body, including lowering cortisol and increasing serotonin. This is why the benefits are so substantial.

Whether it is journaling for five minutes each morning

---

12 Positive Psychology Progress (2005, Seligman, M. P., Steen, T. A., Park, N., & Peterson, C.) Counting Blessings Versus Burdens: An Experimental Investigation of Gratitude and Subjective Well-Being in Daily Life

13 Gratitude Uniquely Predicts Satisfaction with Life: Incremental Validity Above the Domains and Facets of the Five Factor Model

or evening, taking a moment of gratitude before a meal, or writing a thank-you note to someone who has been kind or helpful, each and every thought and act of gratitude shapes the brain and tones the heart. It's easy to become accustomed to our blessings, as human beings are naturally adaptable. For this reason, we can become immune to experiencing our financial security or wealth, our health, or our devoted relationships in a way that stimulates the continual feeling of gratitude, similar to how we felt when we first actualized or became in touch with these gifts of our human experience. It requires intention, and the more we build a gratitude practice, the more it kicks in when we need it. Oftentimes, gratitude is the body's response to the need to ground or drop out of a worrisome or stressful place. It becomes low-hanging fruit for the moments we need to reframe things with a shift in perspective and can literally pull us out of a dark hole. When gratitude becomes a habit, without even realizing it, we find ourselves thinking about what we're grateful for, because that is the pattern or groove we have created in our brain. I think of it as the gratitude imprint, and I work with this practice consistently in my own life. I also model gratitude for my children daily by expressing feelings of thankfulness out loud, be it for a meal, for an opportunity or experience, or for them. It makes me feel good and makes them feel good, and I believe it keeps them grounded in a value system that supports happiness and well-being.

Through practice we are able to cultivate gratitude as an internalized coping mechanism, breeding an emotional and chemical climate of resiliency, greater peace, and equanimity. This brings us back to gratitude repeatedly as the feel-good experience in our bodies and minds that is worthy of our craving.

JOURNALING

So often, we operate on autopilot, and moments of reflection help us make thoughtful choices and evolve in our lives.

In my twenties and early thirties, I journaled all the time. Journaling created that space and time for me to think and feel, and it played a big part in my own personal psychospiritual development. I learned to understand my own mind and my challenges. Reflection through journaling was introspective and ultimately self-affirming in a way that enabled me to integrate the teachings from many life experiences, because I made space for that integration through my writing practices.

In that time in my life, I was consuming an enormous array of teachings from the Eastern traditions. I was studying wellness and spiritual practices and making connections with how they interface with medicine and psychology. At the time, the elective practice of journaling was equally as powerful as all the other work that I was doing in terms of study, practice, and meditation. I could not have internalized, integrated, and made the connections that were needed for my journey ahead without the reflective practice of journaling during those formative years. This was the seed of my knowledge base that I have been further cultivating through years of practice and working with others.

Different styles of reflection work best at different stages of our lives. I stopped journaling when my children were babies because with little space and time for self-care, I fell out of the habit. In hindsight I believe that maintaining the practice would have served me as a new mother in the same way that I processed the wisdom teachings of the East, but this time it would have been about the wisdom experiences of motherhood and the obstacles on that road. Today, my kids are older, and I have brought journaling back into my daily routine. It's a five- to ten-minute block before bed, which has reconnected me with the power of this tool. It feels as though I am making space for my thoughts and feelings at a stage when much of my time is focused on the well-being, thoughts, and feelings of others, both personally and professionally. The fluid feeling of writing with pen and paper also feels great after typing or banging away on my phone all day.

On top of that, the digital age has catapulted us into a

stressful, constantly reactive state, and spacious reflection is a remedy that can counterweight the liabilities of this day and age. Reflection has an entirely different quality than multitasking, which research shows is ineffective anyway. In an article published by the American Psychological Association titled "Multitasking: Switching costs," the authors explain,

"Psychologists who study what happens to cognition (mental processes) when people try to perform more than one task at a time have found that the mind and brain were not designed for heavy-duty multitasking. Psychologists tend to liken the job to choreography or air-traffic control, noting that in these operations, as in others, mental overload can result in catastrophe."[14]

The landscape is fast and crowded in our minds. Whether it's to save lives, increase productivity, or find greater well-being, practices that support our focus and attention are vital. Fifty years ago, people who studied meditation and breathwork were on a spiritual path. Those practices have become a required tool kit, a prescription to address the stress of the twenty-first century and help us avoid catastrophe, however we define it. In the next chapter, we look at the benefits of meditation and the many forms it takes.

---

14   American Psychological Association. "Multitasking: Switching costs." March 20, 2006. https://www.apa.org/research/action/multitask

Chapter Five

MEDITATION

Mark Newman is an optimizer. Despite chronic, severe back pain, he called me to schedule time with a meditation teacher because he wanted to tap into the "superpowers" of meditation. He wanted better concentration, sharper mental performance, and a more acute memory. He was curious to experiment with different forms of meditation to see how each made him feel and how they impacted his output at work and his competitive edge amidst a pool of brilliant colleagues. I explained that to fully understand the impact, we needed to dedicate time to a consistent practice. While it's true that we can try something and immediately feel that it doesn't resonate, gathering information about the potential true impact required deeper work. Mark approached the initial meditation sessions as a way to determine which forms he was attracted to and which he had an aversion to. However, he was insightful enough to understand that sticking with a practice that he may have initially felt an aversion to could have value. There are times when our negative responses are signposts to direct us toward what we need, and there are other times when those reactions are meant to be observed, felt, and eventually overcome. Resistance or fear can be there to protect us, or it can show up as an obstacle that we are meant to face head-on. It's not always easy to tell, and deep listening and exploration of this can be needed in order to know when it's time to choose another method, practice, or approach, and when we must plow ahead.

Unlike many of my clients, who display vulnerability with me, Mark was voracious and confident. He was looking for answers. He would ask me whether I thought a certain practice had the potential to shift his thinking. He wanted specifics about how long he should meditate and how often. He wasn't comfortable sitting on the questions, which is part of the path of meditation. He wasn't looking for practices that would help him open up but rather practices that would give him an edge. I believe his meditation fantasy was that he would sit in a disciplined way for a short amount of time and feel as though he "leveled up" his performance and eliminated his blind spots. He wanted to feel like a superhero.

Nonetheless, because our approach is to meet people where they are, we agreed to try different practices. As it so often happens, the reason he thought he came for meditation was different than why he needed meditation. In the beginning, I wanted to build trust with him, so I let him call the shots. After all, this was his journey, not mine, and I don't pretend to have all the answers. We tried many forms of meditation and talked about the experience after each session. His questions after each session showed me that he was anxious, looking for the right medication instead of meditation.

We reached a point of trust that allowed me to tell him that meditation, like yoga, wasn't going to transform his life immediately, although research has shown that the impacts can be felt in a matter of weeks.[15] Regardless, it's a path that requires a beginner's mind of not knowing. The secret to meditation, which is a hard pill to swallow for many, is that in order to experience the proven effects, meditation requires consistency, commitment, dedication, and repetition, without expectations of arriving somewhere. Only then will the benefits reveal themselves. Patience and persistence is worthwhile as "a large body of research has established the efficacy of mindfulness-based interventions in reducing symptoms of a number of disorders, including anxiety (Roemer et al., 2008), depression (Teasdale et al., 2000), substance

---

15   B.K. Hölzel, J. Carmody, M. Vangel, C. Congleton, S.M. Yerramsetti, T. Gard, S.W. Lazar. "Mindfulness practice leads to increases in regional brain gray matter density." *Psychiatry Research*, January 30, 2011; 191(1): 36–43. https://www.ncbi.nlm.nih.gov/pmc/articles/PMC3004979/

abuse (Bowen et al., 2006), eating disorders (Tapper et al., 2009), and chronic pain (Grossman et al., 2007), as well as improving well-being and quality of life (e.g., Carmody and Baer, 2008)."[16] Meditation and mindfulness practices literally change our brains and in turn impact every aspect of our lives.

Mark has expectations, so patience wasn't the answer he wanted to hear, but he was intellectually willing to understand that meditation is about spacious focus, not laser-sharp and goal-oriented. While meditation may be the secret weapon to the superpowers that he's looking for, those superpowers probably won't show up in the way he expected. A beginner's mind was not something he could easily grab onto.

As he built trust in us and felt himself learning about things he didn't already know, his anxiety lessened, and patience increased. We practiced a combination of breath-based mindfulness and yoga nidra, which is a type of meditation that incorporates body awareness (and will be explained more fully in an upcoming section). At first Mark thought he should practice twice a day for twenty minutes, and he tried. He found consistency challenging in this format due to family obligations, which felt defeating, and he was self-critical about this perceived failure—not the point of meditation, of course. We agreed

---

16 Ibid.

that once a day would be a great place to start and that setting aggressive but realistic goals was best. While a stretch for his super type A personality, it felt healthy for Mark to give himself a break and choose a middle path as he explored the practice. After three or four months of consistent practice, once daily for twenty minutes, he began to experience the benefits of a meditation practice, but not necessarily in the way he thought he would. Mark found himself less reactionary to his thoughts and his colleagues, more present and compassionate in his conversations, meetings, and phone calls, and with less anxiety. An added bonus was that his back pain decreased. As he released his anxiety and was able to dwell in his body, his physical tension lessened.

Over time, meditation helped Mark connect to his body. When he first came to Namaste, I could tell that he was disconnected and disembodied, but my suggestion to combine yoga with a meditation practice fell on deaf ears. After about nine months of meditation, he was open to adding gentle yogic movement. Then, after six months of yoga practice, he said he wanted to start thinking about how he ate. I'm not a nutritionist or dietitian, but I did tell him I thought he should eat in a way that felt nourishing, mindful, and good for his body. He worked with a nutritionist on my team who helped him use food to both care for himself and "level up" at the same time. Mission accomplished.

We had started with meditation because that's what he asked for. Meditation helped Mark open the doors to the other pillars. He was able to find alignment with a different perspective of what meditation could mean for him and came to understand that meditation was more of a journey than a destination—and he found that journey interesting and rewarding. As an aside, Mark's wife sent me a note about a year into his work with us explaining how he was "like a different person" at home. More patient with his children, more unplugged on the weekends, and more present in their love life. She was grateful.

MEDITATION AS MEDICATION

Many people come to us to learn meditation in order to lower or manage their stress. When Yogananda first traveled to the United States in the early twentieth century, people were curious about esoteric topics like yoga and meditation. Many were moved to learn to meditate as part of a journey on a spiritual path. In the last several decades, and particularly since the digital age has dawned, people have taken a secular approach to meditation, seeking mental health and stress management in place of enlightenment. As mentioned, people who meditate benefit from these practices with deep spiritual origins to face real, everyday life problems.

In my twenties I spent a lot of time at a Zen center in

Cambridge, Massachusetts, meditating for many hours each day. At the end, each person was called in to meet with the Zen master, who asked a question called a koan. I felt that I should have an answer, but regardless of the question itself, the answer this Zen master wanted from his students was this: *don't know*. It turns out that *was* the answer. Meditation, at least for me, helps me sit with the spaciousness of not knowing, which can feel like a void in the beginning. It enables me to let go of the need to have control and find my way into the present moment with less anxiety and "holding on."

Many people come to Namaste with the idea that meditation is a magic pill that will eliminate stress and inspire happiness and high performance. While meditation can have that effect, it's a practice that supports us in getting to know our own mind, which enables us to navigate our lives with greater awareness. We return to meditation again and again, and it's a journey that will ebb and flow through the different seasons of life. My clients are often focused on solving problems in linear fashion, and this way of getting things done seemingly works for them in many areas of their life. Their strength can become their greatest weakness, however, when the very way of being successful is also the cause of distress and a less-than-fulfilling experience of their life. Opening up to a different way of thinking can be scary, especially when our modus operandi has served us well, until it doesn't.

FORMS OF MEDITATION

Oftentimes, actions precede feelings. If we wait for the inspiration to do something—exercise, meditate, write a book, learn to paint—it may never happen. In the beginning, we may have to apply a "fake it till you make it" mentality because it is the practice itself that will manifest the inspiration and feelings we are looking for. When my alarm goes off at 5:30 a.m., I don't necessarily want to get up and begin my morning routine that includes meditation, but it is the memory of the feeling that yesterday's practice gave me that convinces me to do it again today. I know my morning practice will make my day feel exponentially better. I "just do it" and I'm always glad I did.

There's not one kind of "right" self-care routine that works for everyone. Instead, it's important to create practices that are enjoyable and right for us based on our needs, goals, interests, and stage of life. Self-care shouldn't be one more thing on our to-do list, but rather woven into our life until it becomes part of the fabric itself. But the fabric of our life changes, and the practices will change and be expressed differently as we move through ages and stages. My practice today—with a family to care for and a business to run—is different than the practice I had in my twenties, when my life was more carefree. I imagine that it will continue to evolve as I age.

One of Namaste's clients, Jessica Strong, who is the

CEO of an extremely large tech company, has a standing Sunday evening appointment with a meditation teacher. While mindfulness is the foundational practice, the meditation style can shift depending on what she needs in her life. It's her mindfulness practice that has enabled Jessica to develop the ability to listen deeply to her thoughts and feelings, and on days when a Metta (loving-kindness) practice is called for, or a restorative, guided practice is most supportive, she knows how to give herself what she needs. If we meditate once a week or one minute a day, it's a beautiful place to start. This type of quiet, sacred space is scarce for many people who are not engaged in organized religion or a spiritual community, and something is always better than nothing. Whether we feel aligned with the idea of organized religion or not, going to church, going to temple, or engaging in daily prayer is a time-out from the daily grind. If those observances are not built into our weeks, it makes the need for creating space for quiet stillness even more important, in my opinion.

There are many places to enter a meditation practice. The various schools and full scope of meditation practices are too numerous to list here, but we can look at some general types of meditation. Remember: just because we learn one style doesn't exclude the others, although going deep with at least one practice will serve our exploration of others. After having meditated for over twenty-five years, I often find myself using a meditation that best fits my mindset that day. While my foundational practice is a breath-based mindfulness practice, if I'm feeling extra anxious, I might work with a guided visualization; if I'm feeling distracted, working with a mantra or using prayer beads can help me focus.

BREATH-BASED MINDFULNESS MEDITATION

Breath-based meditation can be the simplest and most challenging practice. During a breath-based mindfulness practice, we sit upright, our spines straight and long, but without rigidity. Our eyes can be closed or softly open, gazing on a spot on the floor a few feet ahead. At first, as we breathe normally, we settle into our body by noticing the physical sensations, the sounds around us, the temperature of the air, and the experience of the surrounding environment. We then come to rest in the awareness of the breath, feeling, observing, and following our exhalations, without controlling the breath itself.

When the mind wanders, as it inevitably will, we watch the thoughts without judgment. When a thought arises— like *Oh, shoot, I forgot to send that email*—we label it "thinking" and let it go, returning to the breath. Every time the mind wanders to a thought, we label it "thinking" and return to the exhalation. We simply notice our thoughts without becoming identified with, reactive, or attached to them. It's natural for the mind to wander. We work toward bearing witness to the patterns of our mind without judgment.

BREATHWORK AND PRANAYAMA

Breath is our life force, which makes breathwork an incredible practice. Inhaling is the first thing we do when we're born, and upon death we sigh one last exhale as if our whole existence is contained in that one lifelong breath.

Breathwork bridges mind, body, and spirit. I like to think of breath as connecting us to each other. With each inhalation and exhalation, we're sharing a giant breath of air with each other, giving and receiving the universal life force.

Many of us have a tendency to disconnect from our breath or hold our breath, and as a result, we're disconnected from our life force and from each other. We can reconnect to our breath through movement such as yoga and through pranayama and meditation practices.

Breath can be an anchor for cultivating mindfulness. By resting our attention on the breath, we can stay present in our minds and bodies in any moment. Many energy practices from Eastern meditative and yogic lineages use specific, focused breathing practices that create a sense of calm, clearing, or infusion of energy.

The ancient practice of pranayama is a powerful meditative exercise. We count and hold the breath—for example, counting to five on the inhalation, holding the breath for two counts, then counting to five on the exhalation. Another practice follows alternate nostril breathing, where we inhale through the left nostril and then exhale through the right nostril, inhale through the right and then exhale through the left.

The "breath of fire" is an energizing pranayama practice where we exhale rapidly through the nose while contracting the belly. These powerful energetic practices are best learned from a teacher. A live teacher brings a dimension to the experience that has been a part of the oral lineage for thousands of years. These practices have a life force unto themselves, and learning in the presence of a pulse helps infuse the power of ancient wisdom at our back.

MANTRA MEDITATION

Mantra meditation is powerful. While traditionally it is a Vedic meditation path, the modern practice has become more secular. In mantra meditation, a word or phrase is repeated out loud, chanted, or said internally. It can be a Sanskrit word, an energetic word, or an affirmation we create, such as "I am light" or "I am brave." In practices like Transcendental Meditation (TM), a teacher gives a student a personal Sanskrit mantra to use during meditation that has a powerful energetic resonance.

The mantra provides something more concrete to rest our attention on than the breath, and the rhythmic recitation of a mantra reinforces deep, fluid breathing. Specifically, mantra meditation can be a balm to anxiety or panic attacks, as it gives us something to focus on in challenging moments.

A vocal meditation can be a simple as saying, "Ahhhh" during an exhalation.

GUIDED MEDITATION AND VISUALIZATION

During a guided meditation or visualization, the teacher speaks soothingly, often describing a beautiful, peaceful location or a journey such as a walk in the woods through spoken imagery. In some cases, we may meet a warm and nurturing maternal figure, a spirit animal, or a guide who shares wisdom. We may tell people who are struggling with stress to take three to five minutes to close their eyes and visit a place that represents calm or happiness in their world. Connecting with the feelings that are conjured up by this "happy place" can help us expand and soften our experience in the moment, which can feel very narrow and constricted. Simply visualizing and connecting with a place that cultivates positive, spacious feelings can enable us to feel calmer, more connected, and in alignment, giving us the strength to navigate the challenge on our plate.

Guided meditation can also work with the chakra system (mentioned in chapter two in the discussion of yoga and asanas), which comprises the seven energetic points from the base of the spine to the crown of the head. The visualization can be intentional, such as drawing a ball of light up through the central channel of the body and ultimately releasing it as streaming light through the top of the head. With knowledge of the chakras, a practitioner can see or feel where the light dims or is blocked, which indicates an energy block that can be worked through and released with the support and guidance of a teacher.

YOGA NIDRA

Yoga nidra focuses on the sensations of the body, using the physical body to access a sense of embodiment as well as relaxation. While lying on our back, we bring awareness to every corner of our body by contracting and relaxing different parts from head to toe.

Some meditation relaxes our mind to relax our body; other times, as with yoga nidra, we relax our body to relax our mind. The practice is both a release and a tool to scan and gather information about where we are holding tension in the body.

Yoga nidra is sometimes called "yogic sleep" because a forty-five-minute meditation session is said to equal three hours of deep sleep.

In both guided meditation and yoga nidra, we witness our experience in a non-judgmental, compassionate way with the intention of relaxing body and mind.

DYNAMIC MINDFUL MEDITATION

Meditation isn't limited to sitting on a zafu (meditation cushion) silently or while chanting Om. Dynamic meditation is a variation of mindfulness, but rather than mindfully watching our breath, we walk mindfully, noticing how our feet touch the ground and how the air feels on our face. We can mindfully fold the laundry or wash the dishes, feeling the warmth of the water and the silkiness of the soap on our hands. Mindful eating includes gratitude for our food and tasting the flavors and textures fully. The key to dynamic meditation is maintaining a sensory awareness to the moment and returning to that awareness when our mind wanders.

GAZING MEDITATION

Gazing meditation is a form that uses an outer focal point, such as a candle, an image, or a beautiful object to gaze on. When choosing an object of attention, we can think of the natural elements—earth, fire, water, and air—and pick something that represents an element we resonate with or feel we need more of in our world. We can even choose an image of an inspirational person who represents compassion, strength, resilience, or patience. We gaze at the object or image for as long as we are able. When we feel the need to close our eyes, we hold the image in our mind with eyes closed, right between our eyebrows. When we're ready, we open our eyes and gaze once again. We have taught this technique of gazing meditation to many adults and children with ADHD and found it to be extremely helpful, which is an outcome research supports.[17] It is great as part of a tool kit to manage attentional challenges and develop new patterns in the mind in support of better focus.

METTA MEDITATION

This heart-centered or loving-kindness meditation cultivates compassion and connection and is an extremely powerful practice. Silently or quietly, we wish compassion

---

17   H. Poissant, A. Mendrek, N. Talbot, B. Khoury, J. Nolan. "Behavioral and Cognitive Impacts of Mindfulness-Based Interventions on Adults with Attention-Deficit Hyperactivity Disorder: A Systematic Review." *Behavioral Neurology*, April 4, 2019. https://www.ncbi.nlm.nih.gov/pubmed/31093302

and well-being to ourselves, to those we love, to those who are neutral in our life (the dry cleaner, the Uber driver), and to those with whom we struggle. Through Metta meditation, we plant and cultivate the seed to live compassionately in the world. It's a deep and fulfilling practice but can be challenging and even conjure up feelings of resistance, anger, or resentment. Most importantly, remembering to not judge ourselves if our Metta feels less than warm and friendly is important. After all, if we had it all figured out, practice wouldn't be necessary, and all sorts of feelings are par for the course. This "shadow side" is part of the experience, and sometimes we need to move through the less lovely feelings and peel off the layers in order to get to the soft, sweet center.

Although there are many versions, the traditional Metta meditation comprises four statements. One version I like is this:

May I/my beloved/all beings/difficult person be happy.

May I/my beloved/all beings/difficult person be peaceful.

May I/my beloved/all beings/difficult person be healthy.

May I/my beloved/all beings/difficult person be at ease.

Meditation is an oral tradition passed down through a lineage of teachers. Nothing can replace the connection and collaboration with another human, particularly when we're beginning a meditation practice. The teacher creates a tangible and energetic connection to the practice. The teacher also stays with us and guides us when we experience those dark places meditation can uncover.

My own meditation journey began at the Zen Center in Cambridge, Massachusetts. Together as a group we practiced an intense, minimal meditation style with seemingly very little nurturing or support. It made me feel naked and vulnerable, and at that time of my life, I was seeking that kind of challenge and wanted to "bring it on." I was on a spiritual path, seeking connection with something more than my day-to-day existence. When I moved back to New York, I studied Jon Kabat-Zinn, Jack Kornfield, and Sharon Salzberg, and worked with a wonderful teacher named David Nichtern, who is a collaborator of mine to this day. For years, I meditated only in group settings, regularly. I would go to different meditation centers around the city for morning or evening practice and meditated as part of my yoga journey as well.

Today, meditation has become mainstream and fills

a different need than it did twenty or thirty years ago, or a thousand years ago, for that matter. Many people meditate to improve their mental and physical performance, for brain-health reasons, or to manage anxiety and stress, which is wonderful. The downside I see is that for many, meditation has become solely a solitary practice that requires a digital device to execute on. A supportive community and teacher-student live relationship is missing from many people's experience today, especially if we learn to meditate from an app. And while I think apps can be wonderful and very supportive to a consistent home practice, I think when they are the only meditation touchpoint in our lives, something is missing. Meditation is a learning process, a practice that we build, and a relationship in and of itself. It's not easy to sit and watch our breath with all the distractions and stimulations that surround us, and to have the discipline to do that again and again, day after day. Staying curious when difficult moments come up is why we come back to meditation, even on the days it doesn't feel so good. Having a supportive community and teacher helps maintain the curiosity, learning, accountability, and support we need. Like many things, meditation is extremely powerful when it takes the form of a "together action." Yes, apps are an amazing tool and resource to support a practice, and I use them myself, but they're limited because they don't offer the whole experience, which is important to keep in mind.

COMPASSION AND NONJUDGMENT

While we may think of meditation as a mind-based practice, as we learned with Metta, meditation cultivates
awareness in the heart as well, and some practices are
specifically designed for this. Meditation is a mirror for
our state of mind, body, and heart—and looking in that
mirror can be painful and challenging at times. The practice can bring up buried, difficult feelings before we find a
state of calm. We may need to sit with and move through
the shadow side before finding the lightness of being we
are seeking.

If I feel anxious during my meditation morning after
morning, that shows me, like a mirror, that I'm out of
alignment somewhere in my life. I can then look for clues
to what's triggering me. When I witness persistent patterns, this is food for personal development, and I work
hard not to judge myself. Without a meditation practice,
we risk living in a continuous state of reaction or feeling
like a hamster on a wheel. The practice of meditation
shows us where we are fluid and thriving as well as the
patterns we're stuck in—in our relationships, in our jobs,
in ourselves. This awareness serves us over a lifetime.

When I meditate in the morning, I am exponentially
better able to navigate life's daily situations and snafus
from a centered place because I'm less reactionary.
For example, when I'm trying to get my children out

the door for the school bus and feel annoyed because they're moving slowly, I can scream at them to hurry up. Or I can communicate with them by saying, "Listen, I know things are feeling really rushed, but we need to be efficient in order to make the bus." I notice a huge difference in my ability to navigate these moments in a way that I feel proud of when I have started the day with conscious practice as opposed to email or scrolling social media.

At its foundation, meditation is about waking up to the present moment. Intentionally expressing gratitude each day is a mindful practice. We can be mindful when we eat or listen to music. As we build a meditation practice, we find that the practice can easily transfer into moments spread throughout our day.

The beauty of meditation is that we can call on it almost anytime, anywhere, even for a minute or two. Whether it's breathing, gratitude, or loving-kindness, we carry our practice with us amidst a changing landscape. We can be mindful in each of the four pillars, bringing the meditative state to movement, nourishment, and connection.

When we take the time to meditate every day, day after day, there is a distinct ripple effect from every moment of meditation we engage in. We slowly develop a non-judgmental relationship with ourselves, which evolves into compassion and less judgment toward others, and eventually an experience of awakened interconnectedness that has the capacity to change our world and the world around us.

Today, whether we're on a spiritual path, on a high-performance path, or just trying to manage stress and anxiety, these practices support mental health from sanity to deep fulfillment. Rest, reflection, and meditation are foundational to our self-care and enable us to feed our bodies, minds, and hearts for our highest good. This way of feeding ourselves is the third pillar of well-being: nourishment.

THE SECOND PILLAR: STILLNESS
QUESTIONS TO CONSIDER

- Do you pause? Could you pause? If so, can you identify a time in the morning, midday, and evening that this would make sense for you?
- Is where you are placing your eyes and attention in alignment with your values?
- What simple but precious moments of your life are you missing? Could you lie on the grass and stare at the clouds alone or with someone you love?
- What is your favorite way to relax? A good book, cooking a meal, chatting with a friend?
- Maybe you should be doing less, not more? Can you

consider making more space in your calendar for nothing or even boredom?

- Is there a spot in your home or office where you could create a reminder for relaxation by leaving a game or objects that you associate with relaxation out in the open?
- How is your sleep? Are you getting seven to eight hours each night?
- What's happening in your life that needs space? It doesn't have to be grief; are you making space for joy? For love? For reflection?
- Does journaling or a gratitude practice intrigue you? Try one of them for a week.
- Is it time for you to begin to explore a meditation practice?

PRACTICES

- As you start trying to focus on relaxation in your life, leave clues around your home or workspace to remind you of its importance.
- Drop your shoulders, right now. Isn't that better? You probably didn't even notice your shoulders were next to your ears. Now try doing a half shoulder circle—up, back, down—to open the space around your neck and open your diaphragm.
- Try leaving your digital devices outside the bedroom for one night, and notice how much better you sleep.

- Eat mindfully by pausing before your meal to express gratitude, and take the time to notice the smells, flavors, and textures of your food. Breakfast is a great meal to start with, especially if you eat it by yourself.
- As you move through your inbox, practice taking a deep inhalation and a deep exhalation before and after each email. Slow down the process, just a little, and make it more mindful.
- Try this simple meditation: Take a comfortable but upright seat, rest your hands on your lap, and soften your shoulders away from your ears. Softly close your eyes or rest your gaze a few feet in front of you. Begin to notice the sensations in your body, the sounds around you, the feeling of your breath moving in and out of your nostrils. Rest your attention on your exhalation. As your mind wanders, which it will, gently return to your out breath. As it wanders again, come back to the exhalation. Notice the quality of your thoughts, but don't hold onto them or pass judgment. Just return, again and again, to the breath. Do this for one minute or twenty minutes—start where you are.

THE THIRD PILLAR: NOURISHMENT

We are cups, constantly and quietly being filled. The trick is, knowing how to tip ourselves over and let the beautiful stuff out.

—RAY BRADBURY

We're in a constant cycle of giving and receiving with the earth and the universe. Nourishment is integral to this cycle and includes how we feed our bodies, minds, and hearts with breath, food, art, nature, community, sensory experiences, and more.

Connection to our bodies and minds through movement and stillness can tune us in to our needs for nourishment on all levels, including eating a healthy diet. Recent research on the gut-brain connection tells us that how we nourish our bodies not only impacts our mental and physical health but also has the capacity to affect how we age and the diseases we develop, including Alzheimer's disease.[18] The cyclical nature of things means that when we feel nourished, we are inspired to move more, find stillness, and connect with others through touch and connection. We have more to give as well as the capacity for greater creativity and refined output in our work. Nourishment is key in the interplay between the four pillars and caring for our whole being.

Underlying all nourishment is breath, which is also central to a healthy connection with movement, stillness, and touch. Breath is our first exchange with the universe when we are born; it is the one form of fuel that we literally

---

18 Richard S. Isaacson, et al. "Individualized clinical management of patients at risk for
    Alzheimer's dementia." *Alzheimer's & Dementia: The Journal of the Alzheimer's Association*,
    October 30, 2019. https://alz-journals.onlinelibrary.wiley.com/doi/10.1016/j.jalz.2019.08.198

cannot live without. The giving and receiving of breath is literally and symbolically connected to our ability to fill up and give back to the world around us.

Creativity is a cornerstone of nourishment. Consider, for example, how exercise increases tone and circulation in the physical body. In my work I have found that creativity has a similar impact: it tones the mind and the heart and creates the dexterity to create meaningful connections and express ourselves fully.

When we participate in community, we nourish our soul. People need people to be safe and happy. Community supports us through challenging times and shares in our celebrations and accomplishments.

When we nourish and fill ourselves up in a variety of ways, we create a sense of inner abundance.

Chapter Six

NOURISH YOUR BODY: FOOD

My dad has psoriasis and psoriatic arthritis. He takes pharmaceutical medications, which have helped him tremendously and, in many ways, saved his life in that they have enabled him to live well despite a condition that can be extremely disruptive and uncomfortable.

I'd had mild psoriasis since I was a teenager, but after I had my third child, it erupted with a vengeance. The worsening psoriasis was accompanied by psoriatic arthritis, which is an arthritic component to that disease. The arthritis pain left me limping and at times unable to walk without a lot of pain, which was petrifying for me. I had patches of psoriasis all over my body. In many places, my skin was bleeding.

I'd just had a baby, my hormones were at the extremes, it was painful to walk, my skin had open wounds—and I was supposed to be a "wellness expert." Needless to say, I panicked.

I met with Namaste's entire team of nutritionists and many doctors to figure out how to approach it. I didn't want to take the pharmaceuticals that my dad was on, but it was beginning to look like that might be my only option. I researched everything I could find on alternative treatments for psoriasis and psoriatic arthritis. From the information I gathered, I came to the conclusion that I needed to experiment with my diet.

I eliminated dairy, sugar, and all grains including corn and rice. Shortly after I removed those foods from my diet, the disease went into complete and total remission. The patches cleared up, the arthritis went away, and I was able to walk and conduct my life as I had before. Only a few times in the nine years since I changed my diet have I had any sign of the disease—and even then, it's only a small bit peeking through my skin in moments when I'm overly stressed.

I have no desire to eat sugar, dairy, or grains because I feel very supported and taken care of by food and my approach to eating. The changes have been incredibly healing to my body beyond the psoriasis. I no longer suffer seasonal allergies, and my PMS disappeared. I never have to think about my weight because I've eliminated all the foods that make me gain it.

My anxiety has lessened, and I'm able to perform at a level that would be unattainable with my autoimmune disease flaring. With three children, a business to build and run, and a book to write, I need my energy to be optimized. I always have a lot going on (who doesn't?), and I can't afford to have a sugar hangover or feel sluggish and heavy in my body.

That's what worked for me. I believe food is a very personal journey, and I also believe that pharmaceuticals have the capacity to save lives and improve people's quality of life as well. The basics, such as avoiding processed food and refined sugars, are undeniable, and research tells us quite clearly that our gut health is intrinsically connected to our brain and the prevention of many diseases. In addition to the gut-brain connection mentioned earlier, other studies have suggested that the intestinal microbiome plays an important role in modulating the risk of several chronic diseases, including inflammatory bowel disease, obesity, type 2 diabetes, cardiovascular disease, and cancer.[19] At the same time, it is now understood that

---

19   Rasnik K. Singh, et al. "Influence of diet on the gut microbiome and implications for human health." *Journal of Translational Medicine*, April 2017; 15: 73. https://www.ncbi.nlm.nih.gov/pmc/articles/PMC5385025/

diet plays a significant role in shaping the microbiome. Experts have countless opinions on the best diet—vegan, paleo, raw, ketogenic, Mediterranean, etc. Determining our personal path is where science, inner listening, and lifestyle choices meet. It's where food becomes a journey of nourishment that informs our health—body, mind, and heart.

There are some baseline guiding principles that can apply to everyone for mental and physical health. Eating a diet rich in whole foods and nutrients,[20] moderating or eliminating alcohol intake,[21] avoiding refined and saturated fats,[22] and avoiding processed food and sugar are all foundational.[23] However, given the complex nature of our relationship with food, shame around what we put into our bodies is also not a formula for health and well-being. Simply being informed and making incremental progress toward better choices around food is the key.

---

20 Ibid.

21 National Institute on Drug Abuse. "Comorbidity: Substance Use Disorders and Other Mental Illnesses." August 2018. https://www.drugabuse.gov/publications/drugfacts/comorbidity-substance-use-disorders-other-mental-illnesses

22 Maria Fernanda Fernandes, et al. "The Relationship between Fatty Acids and Different Depression-Related Brain Regions, and Their Potential Role as Biomarkers of Response to Antidepressants." *Nutrients*, March 2017; 9(3): 298. https://www.ncbi.nlm.nih.gov/pmc/articles/PMC5372961/

23 Ibid.

FOOD PSYCHOLOGY

Food is family, friendship, culture, and religion. Food is social. It's tied to so many aspects of our lives, our lineage, and our relationships. Food also impacts our mental health quite literally. Given this complex web that is our relationship to food and its role in our lives, figuring out how to nourish ourselves can be confusing.

Whenever my son eats something with red dye, he gets an itchy, swollen, somewhat painful rash. It's not life-threatening, but it is irritating. He's twelve, and he knows he's sensitive to foods with red dye. Still, it's hard when all the other kids at the birthday party are eating the candy from the piñata and he's not, so he eats the candy and suffers the consequences. He's dealing with the psychological issues of preteen peer pressure and wanting to fit in, as well as the emotional and physiological draw of sugar. If I try to control what he puts in his mouth, it seems to complicate things further. I have educated him on the concept of cause and effect, and I do my best to support the healthiest choices possible, but ultimately he needs to hold the control. Like all of us, he has to decide what foods or treats he's willing to give up to feel good in his body, and at the same time I don't want him to feel guilty for wanting sweet treats and to enjoy a piñata with his friends. I work hard to not make him feel bad when he makes a choice that leaves him unwell, but I do encourage him to notice how he feels.

Taking a middle path approach, I educate and advise him to go for the chocolate as opposed to the Swedish Fish at birthday parties instead of no sweets at all, but in the end, he needs to navigate his journey with food, friends, feelings, and health.

If our favorite time of the week is the Sunday evening family dinner and traditionally the meal is pasta, how do we navigate being told we should no longer eat white flour or grains? Multiple generations breaking bread together is deeply nourishing, even if the bread is not what our bodies need. That said, when we remember that it's not only the food that's nourishing, but also the tradition and community that fills us up, we leave space for new traditions that may serve us on every level and leave no damage in their tracks. However, similar to my son and his relationship with a good piñata, some people in this situation might feel as though they'd rather have a couple patches of psoriasis and enjoy pasta with their family every Sunday. If that's true for those people, then it's true. The inner and outer listening gives us an awareness of our choices and the impact they may have on both our physical and mental wellness. I don't believe in perfection.

TWENTY POUNDS OR LESS

Connie Buckley is a top public relations executive in Manhattan with a successful firm and fifty employees.

She worked a lot and, over the course of a decade, slowly went from being a slender size six to a size ten at best. Never much into going to the gym or boutique fitness classes, she came to Namaste wanting to lose twenty pounds through a practice of nutrition, yoga, and meditation. Through her various practices and some supportive wellness coaching, however, she decided she wanted to lose only ten pounds and would be happy there. Losing another ten pounds wasn't worth the effort required to achieve and maintain that weight. She wanted to find a healthy weight that felt sustainable to her, and while her thirties may have been all about size six, she felt comfortable that a size eight in her forties was a reasonable and realistic place to land.

Nourishment is about learning to experience our bodies from the inside out as opposed to the outside in. So often our goals or intentions are inspired by what we want to see in the mirror, or an ideal from the past or the media. Creating goals that are informed by how we feel and that are in alignment with a lifestyle that speaks to us is key to long-term success and a healthy body image. Surrounding ourselves with people who relate to their bodies from an accepting place supports both healthy eating habits and a healthy body image. Researchers from a 2019 study at the University of Waterloo explain,

"Our research suggests that social context has a meaningful

impact on how we feel about our bodies in general and on a given day...Specifically, when others around us are not focused on their body it can be helpful to our own body image...Body dissatisfaction is ubiquitous and can take a huge toll on our mood, self-esteem, relationships, and even the activities we pursue...It's also important for women to know that they have an opportunity to positively impact those around them through how they relate to their own bodies."[24]

As I say to my children, we are the company we keep. People rub off on us, and learning to stay connected to our own core values can be a challenge, so mindfully working with this in our relationships is a process. Awareness is the first step. People, just like food, can nourish us, deplete us, or throw us way out of balance.

A wise and knowledgeable nutritionist can be a tremendous support as we make our way with food, but at the end of the day, we need to make our own decisions about what works for us and what doesn't. Taking personal ownership of the process, gathering information from lab work and doctors, and then listening to our bodies to draw our own conclusions is exponentially more effective than following the latest fad diet.

---

24 University of Waterloo. "Your body image is impacted by those around you." *ScienceDaily*, January 30, 2019. https://www.sciencedaily.com/releases/2019/01/190130075807.htm

My mother has irritable bowel syndrome. She gathered a lot of information and weighed the variables in her life, then made conscious decisions about how to navigate the disease and food in a way that aligns with her preferred lifestyle. She's learned which foods trigger discomfort and which don't. She's made major modifications to her diet and hasn't been able to eliminate the symptoms completely. She could make a full-time job of trying to heal this chronic condition; however, she prefers to focus on the nourishment she receives from focusing on her children and grandchildren, engaging in community, and taking classes on spirituality and religion. My mom has learned to live with a certain level of discomfort as opposed to devoting her full attention to the process of trying to cure her disease. She took information from doctors, naturopaths, and nutritionists and stirred it up with her own vision for her life, creating a middle path approach that feels most authentic today.

Ultimately, it's the integration of the medical advice, the scientific information that we get through learning or bloodwork, lifestyle, goals, values, relationships, traditions, and our intuition that guides us as we navigate our food journey, whether we are addressing a medical issue, a body image issue, or the most optimized approach to nourishing ourselves. How we eat doesn't happen in a vacuum; it is informed by many variables that matter—a lot.

Awareness of the variables in our relationship to food is paramount and enables us to understand the driving forces behind our behaviors and how we're treating our bodies. Where are our choices coming from? Are we motivated by health, weight, culture, food as an extension of our creativity? Our instincts regarding hunger can come from many different places—physical, emotional, cultural, and patterns related to each. We must ask ourselves a simple question: What are we really hungry for? The answer to this question informs how we nourish ourselves on many levels.

In my life, navigating my relationship to food has been an extraordinary healing journey. As a child I felt loved and comforted by my mom's cooking; as a teen and young adult, I felt in conflict with my body and strived for what I thought was perfection, and food became a struggle. Through yoga and meditation, my relationship to my body shifted, and I came to understand food as a tool for health and happiness. As a young mom, the right food became my ticket to having a body that functioned optimally and didn't fall prey to the diseases I was genetically predisposed to. And as a busy working woman juggling many things, food enables me to function at a high level and keep what could be crippling anxiety, exhaustion, and overwhelm from becoming my reality. As with all the pillars we're discussing together in this book, different stages in life call for different approaches. In order to understand what we need at any given stage, we need to be resourceful, be intentional, and practice deep listening.

In short, we gather information and education about what food choices are best for our bodies, consider our personal goals, and blend that understanding with what our bodies, minds, and hearts are telling us. How are we responding to different foods, limitations, and indulgences? Meditation is a beautiful cohort to nutrition, as it is through that practice that we refine our ability to listen compassionately and avoid reactivity, which leads to impulsive choices that may be less than optimal for us.

Informed, intuitive, and mindful nutrition is only one aspect of nourishment. Filling our minds, hearts, and souls with fuel for an internally abundant experience of our lives is also part of total nourishment.

Chapter Seven

NOURISH YOUR MIND: ART

We have many clients with extremely deep pockets, but one stands out in my mind as I think about creativity, art, and nourishment. Judith used a portion of her exorbitant financial resources to purchase extravagant homes and have them decorated by a world-class interior designer. One day she realized that even though the homes were magnificent in their respective designs, she felt like she was living in someone else's houses. She told me that her "houses didn't feel like homes."

She was on a quest for perfection with her real estate investments, but along the way, as a creative soul, she lost her sense of personal expression. When she realized that the lack of creative expression was a void in her life, she chose not to hire an interior designer for a redesign project and put her own creativity to the test. The joy of engaging in the creative process was greater than the risk of choosing furniture that was slightly too big or too small. She played with color and texture and scale in a way that brought her to life and made her homes a canvas for personal expression. These homes that were once thought of as extravagant had layers of feeling, intention, and personal touch that turned them into personal works of art—and perfectly imperfect.

When we fall out of having—or maybe we never developed—a relationship to a creative expression, a part of us is not being nourished. Think about how we educate our children: They have both physical education and art classes in school, as they're both components of becoming a well-rounded, whole being. While humans have been creating since prehistoric times, the less we exercise our creativity muscle, the harder it is to access and use. This poses a problem because in addition to being key to innovation, creativity supports our ability to express feelings and experiences that are too challenging to verbalize, such as feelings about a difficult diagnosis or trauma. In addition, for our high-performance-focused clients, the motivation to engage in creative endeavors, such as learning an instrument, is related to the fact that it has been shown to support mental functioning and white matter connectivity of the right and left hemispheres of the brain. There is plasticity in the brain, and creative endeavors have the potential to support our brain health the way fitness impacts our musculoskeletal health.[25]

Like any relationship or self-care tool, creative expression must be practiced to leverage its gifts. This practice can vary widely from painting, writing, or playing a musical instrument to collage, carpentry, gardening, sewing, and beyond. We all express our creativity in different ways. And just because we're a financial genius and great with spreadsheets doesn't mean we might not also enjoy and benefit from baking or singing.

We worked with a gentleman who used to love to build things. He was a banker by day and a carpenter by night, although he didn't make much time or space for his hobby. This was frustrating for him, but he was having trouble prioritizing this interest in the context of work and family. Building things felt indulgent, yet without the opportunity to work with his hands, he felt an emptiness in his day-to-day. Through his wellness coaching, he got in touch with the importance of making space for creative expression in his life. Together, we agreed that a weekend building project would feel nourishing and therapeutic. Given his need for work/life/family balance, he decided to build a tree house for his children and involve them in

25 Emma Moore, Rebecca S. Schaefer, Mark E. Bastin, Neil Roberts, Katie Overy. "Can Musical Training Influence Brain Connectivity? Evidence from Diffusion Tensor MRI." *Brain Science*, 2014; 4(2): 405-427. https://www.mdpi.com/2076-3425/4/2/405

the project. This was a huge undertaking and, for him, became a bucket-list item. The process of working with wood creatively, using his hands, and putting his tools to work in service of a passion project was both rewarding and stress-relieving for him. Incorporating his children connected the dots in his life, and he was overcome by a sense of fulfillment. When the tree house was complete, he felt like he'd done a good job of parenting, a good job at taking care of himself, and a good job at living. Isn't that a feeling we all want?

LAUGHTER

Humor is creative. Being funny and enjoying funny people taps into intelligence, freedom, and joy and helps us take ourselves and life a little less seriously, which can be a relief. Catherine, a successful investor we worked with, decided to start taking an improv class one night a week. She was known as the "funny girl" her whole life and felt like she had neglected an important side of herself that she enjoyed and took pride in. Life got serious as an adult. After completing this class, Catherine decided to start attending open mic night at a comedy club. She would show up in her blazer and black pants, looking like the businesswoman she was. When she got onstage, she tapped into a source of humor that had been lost since her college days, when she would have her sorority buckled over in laughter at any given party or study break. Catherine had the audience in stitches, and it felt invigorating. Prior to her improv class and open mic nights, her husband was her only audience. She enjoyed being funny, as it felt like a creative outlet for pent-up stress, and her husband enjoyed it, too. He would find himself laughing until he was crying on any given Sunday afternoon, and he needed a good laugh as they were both wiped out from the daily routine that came with having three young children under the age of six. Catherine's humor was one of the reasons her husband fell in love with her to begin with, and Catherine realized that it was one of the things that she most loved and enjoyed about herself.

Making space for fun, whether we are the joke teller or joke receiver, is a nutritious and delightful dimension of the human experience. Like fitness, laughter has been shown to release feel-good endorphins and natural opioids in our brain,[26] and couples who laugh together report greater satisfaction in their relationships. According to a 2017 study in the *Journal of Neuroscience*,

"Modulation of the opioidergic activity by social laughter may be an important neurochemical pathway that supports the formation, reinforcement, and maintenance of human social bonds. In addition to supporting human connection,

---

26 Sandra Manninen, et al. "Social Laughter Triggers Endogenous Opioid Release in Humans." *Journal of Neuroscience*, June 21, 2017; 37(25): 6125–6131. https://www.jneurosci.org/content/37/25/6125

laughter decreases inflammation in the body and our risk of heart disease, most likely because of how it impacts our stress response."[27]

Laughter truly is medicinal. When I talk about feelings following action in terms of self-care, I am reminded of this lovely quote by William James: "We don't laugh because we're happy—we're happy because we laugh."

OPEN TO THE WONDER

There is healing power in the arts, yet many people put creative expression on the back burner when adult responsibilities fill our time and thoughts. Finding practical, realistic ways to reawaken the expression (or create it from scratch if we've never had it before) helps us tone our mind and soul and feel healthier as a human being. Carving out space on our calendars and a physical space in our homes for creative expression helps us mentally hold space for the practice and give it the importance it deserves.

For many clients, creative expression is as simple as taking five to ten minutes each morning to journal or sketch upon waking, or after exercise or morning med-

---

27 L.E. Kurtz, S.B. Algoe. "Putting laughter in context: Shared laughter as behavioral indicator of relationship well-being." *Personal Relationships*, December 2015; 22(4): 573–590. https://onlinelibrary.wiley.com/doi/abs/10.1111/pere.12095

itation. One client told me that she loved to paint as a child but stopped when she was in middle school, when homework and sports occupied her free time. She said she always wanted to paint again.

I said simply, "Why don't you?"

At first, it felt far away to figure out how to bring that practice into her world. I've found that many people harbor a desire for creative process but need practical support to make it real. With this client, we talked about going to an art supply store with a specific list of what she would buy. We identified the space next to her meditation altar as an ideal location for her easel, and ten minutes after meditation as the optimal time to paint. She was able to build the practice as an extension of her meditation practice. When she felt hesitation, she listened to inspiring music to engage her in the work. To fit the painting into her day, she was willing to go to bed twenty minutes earlier so she could get up twenty minutes earlier.

For her, painting was about the process of expressing the range of emotions that bubbled up for her during meditation. She found her artwork, which wasn't particularly amazing to anyone else who saw it, extremely therapeutic. Her painting process mirrored the process of her heart and mind.

The importance of actions that allow us to flex our creativity muscle is backed by science, and even being a viewer of art and creative expression is healthy.[28] In addition to impacting mental health, relationships, and cognitive functioning, studies show that creativity can positively impact physical illnesses such as Parkinson's disease and delay cognitive decline in an aging population.[29] Could engaging in creativity be related to living a healthy, happy life into old age? The Mayo Clinic conducted an extremely compelling study proposing that engaging in endeavors such as painting, drawing, and sculpting as well as crafts like woodworking, pottery, ceramics, quilting, quilling, and sewing during middle and old age may delay cognitive decline. According to the principal investigator, "Our study supports the idea that engaging the mind may protect neurons, or the building blocks of the brain, from dying, stimulate growth of new neurons, or may help recruit new neurons to maintain cognitive activities in old age."[30]

28 Cathy Malchiodi. "Creativity as a Wellness Practice." *Psychology Today*, December 31, 2015. https://www.psychologytoday.com/us/blog/arts-and-health/201512/creativity-wellness-practice

29 Ibid.

30 Rosebud O. Roberts, Ruth H. Cha, Michelle M. Mielke, Yonas E. Geda, Bradley F. Boeve, Mary M. Machulda, David S. Knopman, Ronald C. Petersen. "Risk and protective factors for cognitive impairment in persons aged 85 years and older." *Neurology*, May 2015 ; 84(18): 1854-1861. https://n.neurology.org/content/84/18/1854

RELEASE THE PAIN

Creative expression has the capacity to help us release physical pain and emotional pain as well as process trauma. When we close the door on creative expression or it's simply not a part of our life, we create a block. When we open that door, we invite a deeper understanding as well as a release, which leads to healing and wellness. Many noted physicians have incorporated art therapy into their work. For example, Dr. Bernie Siegel, author of *Love, Medicine and Miracles* as well as *The Art of Healing: Uncovering Your Inner Wisdom and Potential for Self-Healing*, explains how using creativity to understand our deepest beliefs and feelings can enable us to work with those beliefs and feelings in a way that supports our healing process. Dr. Martin Rossman uses guided imagery and tapping into the creative power of the mind for healing the body. In my opinion, whether we engage in creativity with an intentional therapeutic purpose or not, by nature, the fact that we are doing it at all has healing benefits.

In my twenties, I came across a book titled *The Well-Being Journal: Drawing on Your Inner Power to Heal Yourself* (1989) by Lucia Capacchione, PhD. Through this book, I began journaling and drawing as part of my own spiritual wellness and self-care path. The book guides us through a process of coloring an image of our body to articulate where emotion lives in the body. It encourages the use of creativity to understand and heal. For example, if you color your throat black, you may feel you can't speak freely or don't feel supported in your expression. For me, the exercises in the book enabled me to see how my experiences and emotions were living in the cells of my body and, in some areas, creating blockages in my ability to thrive.

FINDING THE TIME

Finding time for creativity is a challenge we all face on some level; we think, *How will I fit this into my life?* In my experience, the easiest way to find time to do something new is to tack the practice onto a part of our life that is already happening, as we discussed in earlier examples.

Our creative expression may be dance, for example, thereby combining movement and nourishment. As I alluded to earlier, one client of ours created a space in her day, while her coffee was brewing the old-fashioned way, to turn on music in her kitchen and dance for five minutes. This simple practice woke her up, brought her joy, served as a creative expression, and helped her go from needing two cups of coffee to one in the morning. Whether we find a pocket where we would normally scroll social media or do busywork, tack creativity onto a movement or meditation practice, make space on a weekend with our kids, or find one night a week to take an art class or participate in an open mic session, with intention and organization it can happen. Similar to movement and meditation, even a few minutes can go a very long way.

KEEP IT HANDY

Rebecca Vischoff had been a client of Namaste for close to a year, but something seemed incomplete about her self-care practice. She ate well, exercised, meditated, and had a solid, intimate connection with her partner. She wasn't depressed, but there was a lack of fullness, a missing element of joy that she had trouble putting her finger on. But through a series of coaching calls, we were able to uncover it. Rebecca said she felt secretly envious of her daughter, who was an accomplished musician living the life of a true artist, and although she had a successful career in Hollywood, it wasn't as creative as she had originally hoped her path would be. We agreed that adding creative expression to her morning practice might help her find an outlet for this value and unmet need, and also bring some playfulness to her days. We gave Rebecca a journal and colored pencils as a gift and encouraged her to use them following her yoga practice. A curious thing happened as a result: Sketching and working with color—although she wasn't a visual artist nor particularly skilled at drawing—ignited an appreciation for creative play. This post-yoga practice became the driving force for getting on her mat each morning, which had been a major tool for stress management while juggling a big job in entertainment and being a mom.

With time, Rebecca's creative practice blossomed further. She bought an easel, huge canvases, and paint. She converted her grown children's bedroom into an art studio and hung her canvases around her, holding her in a creative space she found soothing and inspiring. Her art was only for herself, and provided the perfect balance to her career and actualized a part of herself that felt truly authentic. Rebecca was also able to appreciate her daughter's creative journey once her own needs were met.

As humans, planting the seed for creative energy to expand supports our well-being. We are born to create on some level and bring our unique gifts to the world. Creativity is life, and when this energy is blocked—due to lack of exposure, life's circumstances, or simply feeling that painting/sculpting/writing is for children or professional artists—we can feel less vitality and more stuck. I believe creativity is a tool for longevity as it nurtures our connection to this primal life force, a way to continually give birth. Simply engaging can unlock and open the door to a creative practice that can be both enjoyable and healing. Like any great preschool teacher will say, it's about the process, not the product, and the process supports our development as dynamic human beings.

Chapter Eight

NOURISH YOUR SOUL: COMMUNITY

My daughter goes to Hebrew school, and one Friday evening, she participated in a ceremony where the students were given a prayer book. Parents were encouraged to come to the service and watch. I hadn't been going to Friday evening services because I was often exhausted at the end of a full workweek and chose to take the Friday evening time to cook a meal for my family, giving us the space to gather and reconnect. I usually cooked alone and thought I was just too wiped out to "socialize." This time, however, I knew it was important for my daughter that I be there, and I was looking forward to the meditative space that Friday evening services and prayer can provide.

None of my close friends were there; nonetheless, the room in the synagogue was full of people I knew and had fond feelings for. Everyone shared in prayer and food. When I went home that evening, I felt filled up in many ways. Had I stayed home and cooked alone, I would have missed the opportunity to tap into the power of this nourishing community. As my rabbi once said, "Some people come to services to connect to G-d, and others come to connect with Martin, Josie, or Rachel. They are both great reasons to come!" I experienced the power of both prayer and community, and being in synagogue set the tone for my weekend. I felt supported, safe, and celebrated. This is the gift of community.

I admit that when I complete my work and parenting responsibilities, it can feel like there is a lack of bandwidth for community. This has been an ongoing struggle for me as I recognize the value of these relationships, yet it feels like I have little time and energy to invest. It's hard enough to find time for my nearest and dearest, let alone the next layer of people who, while beautiful in many ways, are more peripheral in my life. Since that evening when my daughter got her prayer book, I recognize that making meaningful space for this type of connection fills me up rather than exhausts me. Leaving my phone in the car and connecting with people and a higher power is worth the push and is exponentially more important than my email, to-do list, or errands.

I have seen through the years the power of community in

times of struggle, as exhibited by the many meal trains I have been a part of for friends who are navigating treatment for cancer or a tough divorce. On the opposite end of the spectrum, community celebrates us throughout the milestones and accomplishments in our lives, which feels great. When my husband and I were considering eloping for our wedding, a wise friend said, "Don't underestimate the power of your friends and family to celebrate this decision and launch you into the next chapter of life. When your community celebrates your decision to marry, they push you forward into this commitment, cultivating a feeling of momentum which is supportive when times are hard or fear sets in." I thought this was so interesting, and it influenced my decision to have a wedding and include the people whose support and blessings seemed valuable to have.

Plugging into community is the opposite of how many people engage today—or, better put, *don't* engage today. Children in the next generation are losing the ability to read facial expressions and body language because they don't look people in the eye when they're talking. A social-emotional developmental shift is happening. Being in community reminds us how, in our often individualistic society, we are connected to the whole. When we connect to community, we cultivate more compassion, we give more, and we certainly receive more. We enter the cycle of life in a fuller way.

SERVICE

Making space for those in need, whether that's delivering a meal to an ill friend or volunteering to mentor a child, brings the cycle of giving and receiving into balance. We tap into compassion and gratitude, and activating those emotions not only makes us feel good, it also changes the plasticity of our brains.

In fact, research indicates that volunteering provides both social and health benefits to volunteers. Those who give their time to people in need have lower mortality rates, have lower rates of depression, and function at a higher level later in life than those who do not volunteer. There is a phenomenon called a "helper's high," and volunteers have more trust in others and greater social and political participation.[31] Sign me up!

I volunteer at my children's school when I can because I like to connect with the teachers, children, and other parent volunteers; helping them feels nourishing to me, so I carve out the time as often as possible. When I get the email about a meal train for a mother in the neighborhood who's going through chemotherapy, I admit my first thought may be, *I feel so bad that they are going through this, but I have no time. I can barely feed my own family,*

---

31   O. Dupuy, W. Douzi, D. Theurot, L. Bosquet, B. Dugué. "An Evidence-based Approach for Choosing Post-exercise Recovery Techniques to Reduce Markers of Muscle Damage, Soreness, Fatigue, and Inflammation: A Systematic Review With Meta-Analysis," *Front Physiology*, April 25, 2018; 9: 403. https://www.nationalservice.gov/pdf/VIA/VIA_fullreport.pdf

let alone someone else's family. But that thought is quickly followed by the moment of clarity: I think, *I have to bring dinner to this family because I truly do care, and because I'm a responsible member of the community. It's not all about me, and someday there may be a meal train for me.*

Remember, actions come before feelings. We care about things we invest time and energy in; how we care about our own children is a great example of this, and sometimes we have to *first* invest the time and energy to *build* the feeling of caring. Engaging in service cultivates feelings of compassion and connectedness, which then drive us to repeat the behavior. At the end of the day, community creates the feeling of abundance from which true inner wealth springs forth.

Many of our clients, despite being surrounded by people, suffer in loneliness. They lack and crave more authentic, intimate connection in their lives. When a person has a lot of money and can pay for hired help for most things they need, the cycle of giving and receiving can sometimes be interrupted. They miss the interdependence between members of the community, such as needing to rely on and get support from other moms with driving and childcare, or the opportunity to borrow or lend eggs from a neighbor because sometimes getting to the supermarket is just too much. Community and service meet when someone needs a ride to a doctor's appointment or jumper cables for a dead car battery. In terms of service, when money is not an issue, it can be easy to write a check instead of showing up and giving time. Don't get me wrong—the donations are extremely important, but serving with our hands, hearts, and minds is a fulfilling practice that leads to a connection with the understanding that the world is bigger than we are. When life is only about us, we miss out on the opportunity to experience the web of community and service, and loneliness ensues.

Ethan Nichtern, a Buddhist teacher and writer who I have known for several decades, talks about the importance of interdependence. As a species, we are all interdependent and interconnected. When we can tap into the sense of interdependence and interconnectedness, it has the potential to manifest feelings of compassion. As Ethan explains in his book *The Road Home: A Contemporary Exploration of the Buddhist Path*, "When we are mindful, we experience our social presence as a series of momentary connections with one other being. These moments of interpersonal connection are like the Lego building blocks of our social awareness." In my experience, this social awareness leads us to compassion.

Many of our clients, because of their position and wealth, sit on the boards of schools or nonprofit organizations. One client told me that she wanted to engage in a more direct way than simply writing a check because she felt out of alignment with the recognition she received without having made any sacrifice in the spirit of service. In our conversation, I suggested that she volunteer at the school instead of, or in addition to, raising money by inviting her friends to a table at the fundraising gala. Through her volunteer work with the students, she discovered that the school lacked an adequate art space and what she considered to be adequate creative resources, something she would never have learned by simply giving money. Her family donated funds to build an art center for the school, donating far more than they normally would have. Her hands-on engagement gave her a greater sense of fulfillment. She also chose to resign from several boards that were draining her energy, so she could have more time to focus on those that were most meaningful to her. She decided that going deeper with her service felt more nourishing than going wide, so to speak.

The commonalities we share as humans—our love for our children, our desire for health, well-being, security, and abundance—are far greater than our differences. When we connect with people in service, we experience the common threads within humanity. Service creates wellness on a macro level, contributing to the wellness of the world. We're inextricably connected to the macro, and when we make the world around us better, we are better able to be healthier ourselves.

Community is the web of interdependence in which we lose our self-absorption and can experience ourselves as part of the whole instead of the whole. Community efforts allow us to express shared values in action, whether it's a PTO event or service with others.

The fourth pillar of touch, which we'll explore next, is where we express ourselves through physical connection and intimate relationship. It's where we see and are seen by other individuals.

THE THIRD PILLAR: NOURISHMENT
QUESTIONS TO CONSIDER

- What nourishes you other than food?
- What one food or habit are you willing to give up in order to feel better?
- What's not worth giving up?
- Do you spend time doing something unfulfilling (like scrolling social media) that could be replaced with something creative? Even for ten or fifteen minutes a day?
- Is there a creative endeavor you've always wanted to try? Or perhaps something you did as a child but abandoned in adulthood?
- Are you part of a community? Were you at one time? Could you return?
- Do you find small, meaningful ways to give back or be

of service? If not, is there someone who could benefit from your support?

PRACTICES

- Consider making time for a home-cooked dinner with your family or good friends at least once a week.
- Eliminate processed foods from your diet (i.e., anything that comes in a wrapper) and refined sugar for one week, and see how your body and mind feel.
- When's the last time you listened to live music, went to a museum or gallery, or took a class or workshop? That long, huh? Make a plan for something fun and inspiring—today!
- How might you begin in a creative project you've been putting off? Take one small step toward making it happen. Make a physical space, collect materials, etc.
- Take one activity off your calendar and say *yes* to a volunteer opportunity. Serve at a shelter, give time instead of money, do something kind for someone in your community, even if you are a bit resistant. Greater inspiration will follow the action, I promise.

THE FOURTH PILLAR: TOUCH

It's also helpful to realize that this very body that we have, that's sitting here right now...with its aches and its plea-

sures...is exactly what we need to be fully human, fully awake, fully alive.

—PEMA CHODRON

When we slow down long enough to actually emotionally, energetically, and/or physically connect with another person, our whole system recalibrates. Whether we are looking into someone's eyes for more than a moment, listening or sharing fully and truthfully, or engaging in therapeutic, platonic, or sensual touch, we are connecting to an important dimension of our human experience.

Touch is about cultivating an awakened heart. When we engage in the pillars—take care of ourselves physically, create space for stillness, and nourish our body and soul— we are priming ourselves to connect meaningfully with others. Otherwise, authentic connection can feel dangerous and vulnerable. Connecting compassionately and mindfully with others can require internal preparation, as the state of our own being informs the quality of our connection, and our connection with others, in turn, is deeply supportive to the state of our being.

Chapter Nine

MASSAGE AND BODYWORK

All of the mental, emotional, and physical patterning from our lives is stored in the cells of our body, contributing to the tension that we feel in our neck and our jaw, the tightness in our low back, or the pain that we feel in our knees. Practices that help us process a lifetime of "stuff" and move it through our physical and energetic bodies are essential. Therapeutic touch helps remove blockages, but touch in and of itself is healing to the nervous system, as evidenced by the fact that this is a major ingredient in caring for healthy babies and children. Human touch of all types is important for soothing stress, creating an experience of social connection, and more. As a scientific report published in 2017 explains,

"...touch-based interventions can improve clinical outcomes in patients with fibromyalgia, rheumatoid arthritis and pre-term infants. Furthermore, social touch has been suggested as a stress buffer, playing a critical regulatory role in the body's responses, including cortisol and heart rate responses, to acute life stressors, which ultimately promotes social connection."[32]

When we engage with massage therapy, we're touching layers of our being, including the mind, musculoskeletal system, emotional body, nervous system, energetic and meridian system, lymphatic system, and more, which is why it has the potential to impact us on so many levels.[33]

Whether we are on a healing journey, or just trying to find balance and avoid injury, massage and bodywork play a role. Consider this: On the one hand, in this day and age, movement and fitness are an important part of people's healthy routine—and that's a great thing. On the other hand, we're exercising with more frequency and intensity than we ever have and doing so well into middle and old age. As a society, we are living longer and need our musculoskeletal systems to maintain vitality without injury. This is all wonderful, but even our fitness routines create a certain amount of muscular tension in the body, and

---

32   M. von Mohr, L.P. Kirsch, A. Fotopoulou. "The soothing function of touch: affective touch reduces feelings of social exclusion." *Scientific Reports*, 2017; 7(13516). https://www.nature.com/articles/s41598-017-13355-7

33   Ibid.

our longevity requires a maintenance plan to minimize pain and optimize function.

Particularly during middle and old age, massage therapy helps address the pain and tension brought on by the patterning that comes from stress, all of life's experiences, and our increased levels of exercise. I frequently get calls from clients who say, "I'm forty-five, and I've been exercising five times a week my whole life. Now, all of a sudden, I have back tension and my legs feel stiff." When I learn they're going to spin class five days a week and sitting at a desk the rest of the time, I'm not surprised they feel tense and tight.

A hard workout is great, but it's not enough to counterbalance the number of hours we likely sit, nor does sitting at our desk, in the car, or anywhere else provide the recovery our body needs. Massage therapy and bodywork are powerful components to an optimized experience of our body. We need to rest and restore our muscles to continue to expect them to perform and produce so consistently.

Massage therapy can impact everything from pain reduction and pain management to mobility, flexibility, the drainage of our lymphatic system, and the release of muscular tension. After a workout, a sport, or a competitive race like a marathon or triathlon, massage therapy effectively relieves extreme muscle soreness that can otherwise show up later on, and it helps refill our well and lessen fatigue after exertion and vigorous exercise.[34]

In addition to physical benefits, massage impacts the mind, too, because as we have discussed, the mind and the body are intricately connected. Massage therapy stimulates pressure points that lead to increased vagal activity, which decreases the stress hormone cortisol and increases immune activity. Massage therapy also increases the feel-good neurotransmitters that thwart the experience of pain and improve sleep.[35] Massage has even been found to be supportive in the management of hypertension, autoimmune disorders, and the process of aging.[36]

Massage is therapeutic touch and a legitimate bullet point on the self-care practice list. I understand massage therapy can seem like a luxury because of the cost involved, but it can be an essential practice for those who expect a lot from their bodies or those who are suffering in some way. When done consistently, massage therapy can act as a mirror for the body, much like meditation can do for

---

34 O. Dupuy, W. Douzi, D. Theurot, L. Bosquet, B. Dugué. "An Evidence-based Approach for Choosing Post-exercise Recovery Techniques to Reduce Markers of Muscle Damage, Soreness, Fatigue, and Inflammation: A Systematic Review With Meta-Analysis." *Frontiers in Physiology,* April 26, 2018; 9: 403. https://www.ncbi.nlm.nih.gov/pubmed/29755363

35 Tiffany Field. "Message therapy research review." *Complementary Therapies in Clinical Practice,* November 2014; 20(4): 224–229. https://www.sciencedirect.com/science/article/pii/ S1744388114000425

36 Ibid.

the mind. We see how our musculoskeletal landscape changes and evolves, and we can catch imbalances before they bloom into injuries. We see where the body is holding tension and address it consistently. Massage and bodywork are productive and reflective. For example, a therapist can give feedback about where we're particularly tense or have limited range of motion. Having that information informs our behavior, like what muscles we choose to stretch in the morning and how hard we exercise that week. In this way, it's an active and interactive part of the self-care experience in addition to being an opportunity to receive and refuel.

In terms of injury prevention, just as the aches and pains increase as we age, our risk of hurting ourselves does as well. The consequence? When we get hurt, we are thus unable to exercise, and we end up being ten times worse off than we would be had we simply been a little more mindful, moderate, and balanced in our overall approach to self-care. Coming to understand the tendencies in our body enables us to behave accordingly so we can sustain a consistent routine without aggravating a predisposition to an injury. Massage therapy, along with the practices in the other pillars, is key because it helps us get perspective on where the body is, what it needs, and what it can do without, like that one last mile on a long run.

For example, when we meditate consistently, we wake

up in the morning and sit in our own skin. We attune our mind to see where we are mentally, emotionally, and physically. We notice the days we feel tired or anxious or inspired. The consistency of meditation practice provides context for the day-to-day experience of ourselves in that practice. Something similar happens with massage therapy and all kinds of bodywork. If we get a massage once a week, that weekly check-in with our body delivers a huge amount of information. This information provides context to the larger landscape of our physical needs and experience.

Massage is an opportunity to plug into and connect to our bodies. It reminds us to feel. In general, all massage is good for pain reduction, circulation, and reducing inflammation. In addition, a sixty- or ninety-minute block of time unplugged is extremely valuable to our high-performing clients who struggle to slow down. Massage downtime enables them to turn their gaze inward, 99 percent guaranteed. The external stimuli will be blocked out, and they'll be forced to be in their own skin—a very healthy practice. It's nurturing to be on the receiving end of touch and energy. So many of us are constantly in output mode at work, with our families, and with social interactions. Receiving refuels our tank.

STUCK IN PAIN

Simon is the third generation to manage his family's automotive business. Guided by a personal trainer, Simon's workout consists of kickboxing, boxing, and combat sports that are physically and mentally intense. When we met, it was clear he was strong, but his body was so rigid that he was in constant pain. Even walking was uncomfortable. The muscular tension showed on his face, and while he could box, he had limited mobility and could barely raise his arms over his head.

To begin, we recommended massage therapy, but Simon wasn't consistent in his practice. He would call when he was in a crisis and get a random massage or two or three. He'd loosen up and feel a bit better, but then he'd go back to doing his intense workouts and training. Inevitably, he'd call us a couple of months later in the same situation. He admitted that he felt mentally and physically stuck at times because of the pain, like he was in a holding pattern. He explained that sometimes it felt like the physical discomfort evolved into mental discomfort, and they would feed off one another in a cycle of tension. While the fitness and boxing were meant to be a release, somehow he felt more tightly wound as his body braced itself in the climate of chronic pain.

Finally, we convinced Simon to incorporate weekly Thai bodywork sessions. Thai bodywork takes place on a mat on the floor, not on a massage table. The practice blew Simon's mind because it enabled him to increase his mobility and release a lot of the muscular tension and pain. In Simon's mind, equally as significant as the pain reduction was the impact Thai massage had on his performance in his different athletic endeavors and personal training. What's more, he felt that the bodywork was opening his mind as it was loosening his body. Simon experienced a quality of ease on a mental level that he had trouble describing but insisted it was all a result of his weekly bodywork. He told me that he would sometimes feel tears running down his face in the shower after the sessions and didn't know why, but it felt good.

I don't think Simon was expecting bodywork to be as impactful as it was. He thought of it as a remedy for his physical pain—which of course it was—but he wasn't in touch with how stressed he actually was. It was only in sessions when his muscles started to soften, and he alleviated some of the tension in his body, that he started to experience a bubbling of emotional release. As long as his body was contracted and stuck—no matter how many glasses of scotch he had—he wasn't able to access a fluid and spacious emotional state of being. His contracted body limited his experiences on many layers.

Consistent bodywork was the key to unlocking Simon's body and opened the door for him to recognize some of the emotional patterning and stress he was experiencing, which of course also contributed to the rigidity of his body. He realized that not only was massage helping him feel less pain and perform better at his sports, but it was also literally making him feel happier. For example, Simon said that he never had the patience to sit with his babies and read stories at night. He'd lie in bed and read to them, but it was hard because he was so wound up and in pain. On the evenings that he would get his massages, he felt like he was a better dad, more able to be relaxed and present with his very young children. Eventually this spread to all the evenings and became the new status quo.

TYPES OF BODYWORK

Bodywork encompasses a wide range of ancient and modern therapeutic touch practices that include massage therapy, Shiatsu, Thai massage, Rolfing, assisted stretching, reflexology, even Reiki. There are more than three hundred methods of bodywork, and I've included a handful here that I'm most familiar with and that we use consistently at Namaste.

Massage therapists often use several different types of massage and bodywork modalities in a session to meet us where we are on both a physical and energetic level. They may address muscular tension, our fascia, and/or our lymphatic system, calling upon different skills and techniques. The massage therapist may also look for energetic blockages or explore where we are holding emotional stagnancy. Then they'll work to open up the flow of energy.

Many think we get bodywork to release muscle tension, but to truly benefit, we have to consider *why* our muscles are tight in the first place. The source of the muscular tension can vary and usually is connected to some sort of physical injury or repetitive stress, mental state, or emotional experience. Energetic blocks result, which impact everything. Using bodywork techniques to release patterning touches the physical, energetic, and emotional planes, moving toward the source of the issue and relief.

THAI BODYWORK

Thai bodywork is otherwise known as "lazy person's yoga" and can be a great solution in lieu of yoga if we physically can't practice, if we don't like to practice, or if we crave more passive stretching and touch. Thai bodywork essentially provides the benefits of massage, yoga, acupressure, and energy work—all rolled into one. It's a combination of passive and somewhat more active stretching, facilitated by a bodyworker and their own body as a tool.

Thai bodywork is like a dance. The practitioner uses their hands, their feet, their limbs, their whole self, and their focus to manipulate our body into different positions that will support a release. Thai bodywork is great when we're dealing with a lack of flexibility or range of motion that is contributing to tension or pain in the body. Similar to acupuncture, it focuses on the meridians in the body. A session typically lasts ninety minutes and is done on a futon mat on the floor. Both giver and receiver wear loose, comfortable clothing.

SHIATSU

Shiatsu is an ancient Japanese bodywork technique that's the massage version of acupuncture, as its foundation is in traditional Chinese medicine. Similar to Thai bodywork, Shiatsu can address back and neck pain, digestive problems, fatigue, and sleep issues, and it calms the autonomic nervous system, which decreases feelings of stress. Shiatsu works on the meridian system, which is a huge number of invisible pathways or lines of energy that run throughout the body. Shiatsu practitioners tap, knead, and stretch pressure points along the meridian lines, with less focus on the assisted stretching and mobility work that happens in Thai bodywork. Shiatsu powerfully clears energetic blockages and stimulates the body to find balance. In a meditative state, the Shiatsu practitioner learns what the recipient's body needs by gathering information through their hands, paying attention to the recipient's circulation, and finding blockages or areas of weakness.

The practitioner is able to stimulate specific meridians, cultivating balance as well as improving circulation of blood and lymph. The meridians tap into many layers of wisdom in the body, and this work is understood to tone the internal organs and strengthen the immune system when done consistently. It is a wonderful adjunct to acupuncture treatment as it builds on and supports the same approach. Similar to Thai bodywork, there's no oil, and it's performed on the floor on a futon in loose, comfortable clothing.

Like pranayama, yoga, and other forms of massage and bodywork, Shiatsu opens up the vital energy channel—the chi—in our body. When we unlock the chi, or internal life force, a feeling of vitality ensues from the inside out, letting go of everything we don't need as well as creating an opportunity to infuse and inspire our body and our mind with a newfound flow of vitality.

Certain forms of bodywork such as Shiatsu are meditative and energetic in nature. While being on the receiving end of these types of bodywork leaves us feeling restored, we aren't taking energy from the massage therapist. The massage therapist is acting as a channel with the intention of enabling us to activate our own internal energy. It's like a jump start when a car battery dies; we need the other car's battery to activate ours, but once it gets activated, we don't need the other car anymore. Bodywork based on ancient practices like Shiatsu or Thai massage awaken our own life force and fuel us for a healthier journey.

In addition to acting as a channel, a skillful bodyworker, whether they're practicing Shiatsu, Thai bodywork, or another form of touch, is both listening to our body and giving at the same time. They're learning from what our body is communicating nonverbally, sensing patterns or any areas of disharmony.

These bodywork practices we've discussed are meant to alleviate stress and tension in the body and restore balance. They approach it from slightly different angles and philosophies, but for the most part, the goal is very similar. In the big picture, there are certain bodywork practices that are Eastern-based and others that are Western-based. Some of the newer practices are influenced by both East and West, and as we discussed, many practitioners incorporate different techniques into a single session to best meet a client's needs.

DEEP TISSUE MASSAGE

Unlike Thai bodywork and Shiatsu, deep tissue work comes from a Western perspective. Deep tissue massage is done on a massage table without clothes and with massage cream or oil. People frequently use deep tissue massage for low back pain or neck and shoulder pain.

Strong pressure is applied in slow strokes to release layers of fascia and muscular tension. Fascia is the connective tissue surrounding the muscles, and oftentimes the fascia holds a lot of constriction. Unlike Thai bodywork or Shiatsu, deep tissue massage focuses primarily on the large muscles. Besides muscle release, according to studies in the *Journal of Alternative and Complementary Medicine* and the *Journal of Clinical Psychiatry*, this powerful technique has been proven to lower blood pressure, reduce stress hormones, and improve mood. Researchers at the Department of Psychiatry and Behavioral Neurosciences at Cedars-Sinai Medical Center have demonstrated that Swedish massage can alter biological markers of immune response as well as hormones associated with stress.[37]

Sports injuries are likely the number one reason people request deep tissue work. Others crave the intensity and the sensation of deep tissue work, which is sometimes painful in a therapeutic way. For these people, I believe the intensity helps them drop out of their minds and into their bodies because the sensation is so strong that they can't be anywhere else. Many clients feel so bombarded by stimulation all day long that they experience the deep pressure as a way to captivate their full attention and land into the present moment.

---

37   Cedars-Sinai Medical Center. "Adults demonstrate modified immune response after receiving massage, researchers show." *ScienceDaily*, September 9, 2010. https://www.sciencedaily.com/releases/2010/09/100908094809.htm

SWEDISH MASSAGE

Swedish massage is a common, traditional Western therapy, with its primary intention to relax the entire body. The technique uses long, fluid strokes to increase the level of oxygen in the blood, improve circulation, and provide muscular relaxation and release. Similar to deep tissue massage, recipients are naked, on a table, with cream or oil. Swedish massage is much gentler than deep tissue and focuses on the superficial muscles as opposed the connective tissues. Swedish massage can also serve as a foundational practice from which a massage therapist can create a prenatal experience, utilize deep tissue technique in select areas, or even introduce tools like hot stones.

REIKI

Reiki is a Japanese energy system and technique based on the idea of the unseen life force energy that flows through everybody. In Japanese, "rei" means high intelligence, and "ki" is energy, like chi or prana; Reiki, then, is the combination of a life force guided by higher intelligence. It is usually done by placing hands on or slightly above the recipient's body. People seek out Reiki for a very wide range of reasons, as the energy activates a relaxation response and promotes healing. When this life force energy is low or depleted, sickness or stress can more easily penetrate us.

A Reiki practitioner goes through a series of initiations

with a Reiki master, which are called attunements. Those attunements are said to open the practitioner's channel in order for them to be a clear conduit for the actual energy work. The practitioner passes life force through their hands onto another person. In order to tap into this energy, oftentimes the Reiki practitioner will utilize or visualize ancient symbols that have the potential to unlock that flow.

CRANIOSACRAL THERAPY

Craniosacral therapy is a subtle, gentle, but powerful treatment utilized by massage therapists, osteopaths, and chiropractors primarily. Generally done on a massage table without oil or cream, it uses gentle touch to shift and manipulate the skull or cranium, the spine, and parts of the pelvis to treat disease by supporting the body's own healing capabilities. It is understood to impact the central nervous system by affecting the circulation of cerebrospinal fluid that surrounds the brain and spinal cord to treat dysfunction and relieve pain. People seek this form of therapy for a wide range of reasons from autism to Alzheimer's, and from back pain to migraines. It also is helpful for good old-fashioned stress and anxiety. There are many skeptics out there when it comes to craniosacral therapy, but in my experience I have heard reports from clients claiming lovely relaxation to total transformation and pain relief. I have also personally benefitted from the power of this work.

LYMPHATIC DRAINAGE

Lymphatic drainage is a popular and somewhat trendy form of medical massage that supports the movement of the lymph fluid around the body. Lymph fluid is a combination of water, waste products, proteins, and other immune system components. Lymphatic drainage is known to have aesthetic and detoxification benefits as it removes toxins from the tissues and supports conditions such as arthritis, fibromyalgia, hormonal imbalances, digestive problems, headaches, and more. These health conditions can interrupt and stagnate the flow of lymph fluid through the body, causing buildup and swelling called lymphedema. Manual lymphatic drainage massage is performed without oil or cream on a massage table, naked, using a variety of motions to stimulate the lymph system.

All told, bodywork provides a channel for us to connect with ourselves, tap into the primal healing power of human touch, and gauge our mental and physical state. In the next chapter, we look at relationships with others as a form of touch and connection.

Chapter Ten

RELATIONSHIP

Samantha Smith and her husband both grew up with divorced parents. They married very young and have a codependent familial relationship, of sorts, with three teenage children. While Samantha's husband has many positive qualities, including being a brilliant and renowned surgeon who has saved many lives, behind closed doors his behavior toward her could be dismissive, and he showed up in their relationship in an emotionally limited and distant way. Yet Samantha was determined to stay married as she had suffered the wounds of divorce and was committed to creating a different family story. She spent a lot of time in psychotherapy working on her relationship with her husband, refining how she responded to him, and while things were challenging, she made the marriage work. After years in therapy, she felt she needed additional tools to manage the stress she held in her body and to continue to evolve how she responded in her relationship. When she came to Namaste, we worked with Samantha to develop a practice of breathwork, meditation, daily movement, and massage therapy. She continually worked on holding strong boundaries, breathwork, and mindfulness so she could respond to her husband from a centered, clear, compassionate place. She mentioned often how her time on the massage table inserted a loving energy into her weeks that felt uncomplicated and nurturing. Samantha held her feelings in her body, and the process of connecting with them and letting them go through a variety of bodywork techniques enabled her to avoid a prolonged somatic response to stress that would cause illness. Her self-care practices combined helped her hold strong, empathic boundaries in her marriage, and see her husband's stress and suffering as his own.

Samantha's self-care practice anchored her and enabled her to actualize her goal of staying married. She leveraged the practices to prime herself mentally, emotionally, and physically, and being in great shape was empowering. She runs for about forty-five minutes each day, practices yoga twice a week with meditation and breathwork, and has weekly massages. While Samantha didn't try to "fix" her husband as her path was her own, after a few years of observing Samantha, her husband was also inspired to work on himself in a multidimensional way. Ultimately, they are both working hard to build self-awareness, strength, and softness. As a result of years of work, they both feel more connected to each other's beauty as well as their own, and more capable of recognizing painful and dysfunctional patterns that separate them from that perspective.

Relationship is our ability see the light in others, and an opportunity for us to be seen as well. There is an imperfect beauty in each of us, and we can move through our day in a vacuum, disconnected and out of touch—or we can cut through indifference and distraction and look to see the good in others. If we can believe it exists and cultivate this lens, regardless of whether we are with our most intimate friends or the dry cleaner, we hold a key ingredient to inner wealth.

OUR GREATEST TEACHERS

The ability to build healthy, lasting relationships is one of the most foundational aspects of mental and physical well-being. Healthy relationships decrease stress levels, help us heal better after surgery, give us a sense of purpose, and can add years to our life. A team at Brigham Young University conducted a meta-analysis of studies that look at the health impacts of social relationships. They reported to Reuters that "a lack of social relationships was equivalent to smoking up to 15 cigarettes a day... and having low levels of social interaction was equivalent to being an alcoholic, was more harmful than not exercising and was twice as harmful as obesity."[38]

As human beings, we need relationships to grow and thrive.[39] Beginning with our mother, the path of relationship provides the opportunity for us to learn about ourselves, learn about others, and evolve through the obstacles we face in life. Surrounding ourselves with people who push us to break through our limitations and overcome obstacles is like medicine, albeit sometimes in disguise. Intimate relationships are not easy and require deep work and commitment in order to bear the ripest fruits.

The more we connect with and learn to accept and love ourselves, the more deeply we're able to connect meaningfully and authentically to the people we love. We return to the four layers of the Metta meditation. The first is our relationship to ourselves; the remaining three are intimate relationships, neutral relationships, and challenging relationships.

---

38 Maggie Fox. "New health policy: encouraging friendships?" *Reuters*, July
    27, 2010. https://www.reuters.com/article/us-lifespan-relationships/
    new-health-policy-encouraging-friendships-idUSTRE66Q6KA20100727

39 Northwestern Medicine. "5 Benefits of Healthy Relationships." *HealthBeat*. https://www.
    nm.org/healthbeat/healthy-tips/5-benefits-of-healthy-relationships

I could write an entire book on this topic alone, and it is a theme woven throughout the four pillars. Our self-talk, or the voice inside our head, is a powerful place to focus when nurturing this realm. The world-renowned researcher Brené Brown talks about how people who wake up in the morning feeling like "I am enough" are the happiest, most wholehearted people. When we are wholehearted with ourselves, we can more readily welcome others into that dimension. The practice of not being hard on ourselves when we make mistakes, the practice of accepting our humanity and imperfections lovingly, yet still growing and evolving, is self-love. But where to begin? Simple rituals are a great start. Our hands are an extension of our heart. Take a moment to try this:

Place your hand on your heart, right now. What are you feeling? What are you thinking? Offer love inward by telling yourself that you are enough. Breathe for just one minute, repeating the mantra "I am enough" or another affirmation that feels right. You can also put your hand on your belly, where your power center is. The feeling there is slightly different than putting your hand on your heart. Your affirmation for this practice may be "I can be honest and brave," focusing on tapping into your inner strength. Now try putting one hand on your heart and one hand on your belly. You connect with your compassion energy and your power energy simultaneously.

Another more active expression of this idea that I learned from the renowned neuroscientist Wendy Suzuki is a mind-body fitness practice called intenSati. Developed by a woman named Patricia Moreno, the name is derived from the word *intention* and a *Sati*, which is from the Pali language of India and means "awareness." The practice combines intense bursts of movement from a variety of practices like martial arts, yoga, and dance with the shouting of empowering affirmations such as "I am strong" and "Yes, I can!" Combining empowering movements with inspirational words is transformational and helps us diminish negative beliefs about ourselves.

Whether we resonate with a quieter, more heart-centered affirmation practice or a physically and mentally intense and empowering practice—or both—when practiced regularly, these affirmative rituals water the seeds of self-love and self-confidence, and melt away self-destructive patterns.

INTIMATE RELATIONSHIPS

Our most intimate relationships are the laboratory for our personal growth. Through those relationships, both wounding and healing take place. Here, we learn about and can practice being human. We learn to express our needs, accept the imperfections of others, apologize, and learn about commitment. Our families of origin as well as the families we create through partnership, marriage, and procreation are fertile ground for these challenges and growth opportunities to present themselves. Within these primary relationships, we are faced with the puzzle of finding intimacy, forgiveness, and acceptance despite differences and sometimes dislike. Siblings can push each other's buttons and force each other into growth through conflict and resolution, and through learning to communicate honestly and compassionately, which sometimes comes after heartache and pain. The opportunity for healing is always there, but sometimes we have trouble peeling off the layers to get to the vulnerability that leads to repair.

Intimate relationships are our greatest teachers when we approach them with openness, curiosity, and intention. By creating practices within our relationships that anchor us in the intention of love, learning, and connection, similar to a self-practice that serves that purpose as described earlier, we set the stage for fulfillment, which does mean perfection. For example, consider the hugging practice I have with my children. Each day as part of our morning routine, which can sometimes feel very stressful and time-crunched, I hold them with intentionality and take a full breath. It's quick, and they barely notice. For me, it's a touchpoint that centers my day, reminding me what is most important in my life. Prioritizing moments for intimate connection, whether it's hugging our child or making love to our partner (instead of binge-watching Netflix), bears fruit. This is the fruit of commitment to move through the hard stuff, anchored in the intention to nurture connection. It can be ugly, no doubt, but this is the nature of the human experience, the shadow side of everything magnificent and worthwhile.

NEUTRAL RELATIONSHIPS

Those with whom we have a neutral relationship are an opportunity to practice honor, respect, and reverence for other humans. Interestingly, but not surprisingly, often with these people we are able to access and feel an easier expression of heartfulness than we can with our closest relatives. Why? One reason is that they do not push our buttons the way intimate relationships do, and they enable us to rest wholly on our values and teachings, as opposed to being sidetracked by emotional responses. Making an authentic connection in the moment with people such as our taxi driver, the front desk assistant at a doctor's office, or the barista at our favorite coffee shop is healthy on many levels. In that moment of connection, we feel our humanity, and it engages us more deeply in the experience of living. Taking a moment to see and recognize the humanness of someone who sits in this "neutral" relationship category creates a namaste experience. By "namaste experience," I mean the ability to recognize that every human holds a divine light within them; the term *namaste* acknowledges this principle, as do words and beliefs from many other spiritual traditions.

CHALLENGING RELATIONSHIPS

Tapping into the universal, evolved experience of love allows us to navigate those more challenging relationships with mindfulness and a more malleable heart. When we can't move through a challenging relationship, we suffer. This stagnancy has the potential to manifest mental and emotional hardship as well as physical illness. The pain that festers in the dysfunction, anger, and even rage that lives in these challenging relationships can produce even greater pain, or healing, depending on how we work with it. We move through this difficult place and grow when we approach the tough relationships with some awareness of our own story line. The ability to bear witness to a situation from a more spacious and objective place enables us to communicate more mindfully without getting stuck or swept into a negative vortex of mind and heart.

To the extent that we can learn to listen in these relationships and let them be our teacher, they will serve us on the path to inner wealth. Personal growth and true fulfillment require obstacles to build stamina and flexibility, which ultimately enable us to feel strong and happy from our core.

"I don't know what you're doing, but something has really shifted since she started working with you." Colby Parker's chief of staff spoke those words to me a few months after I'd begun working with the socialite. This was the late 1990s, and yoga was becoming more mainstream. Colby had read a *Vogue* article about a supermodel who practiced yoga. She came to yoga to be cool, stay thin, and have toned arms for her sleeveless ballroom gowns. We met her where she was—let's get those arms toned! In the meantime, we added breathwork and mindfulness practice, and snuck in a three-minute simple guided Metta (loving-kindness) meditation at the end of the session.

Before she began practicing yoga, Colby was indifferent to the incredible team of people who worked in her home—not abusive, but not reverent either. She paid more attention to her nails and page six of the *New York Post* than she did to the people who made every aspect of her life work seamlessly, daily. After about six months of yoga, breathwork, and meditation three times a week, something shifted. Colby began to look her helpers in the eyes, smile and say hello, and even ask how they were as part of a morning greeting. The entire energy of the house shifted because her vibration was different, and her dedicated team felt that shift in a big way.

Colby jokingly said to me during one of our sessions,

"I'm becoming a better person every day because of you." Even though she laughed it off, it was really happening. Her friends and family asked her why she seemed softer and more easygoing. She admitted that while she didn't think she had changed much, the work we were doing did make her think about things a bit differently.

RELATIONSHIPS ARE THE KEY TO SUCCESS

Dave Sutter had been practicing yoga and meditation three mornings a week for about a year when he decided to create a wellness program for his employees. He told us the work we'd done had such a profound impact on him; he was able to think more clearly and creatively, navigate big decisions with less anxiety, and overall feel like a happier human being. Dave wanted his employees to have the same experience, too. His interest was, of course, in having productive, loyal employees, but he also wanted them to have a better experience of being at work and live their best lives. He attributed these more altruistic motivations to his own yoga and meditation practice.

The program, one of the first corporate wellness programs Namaste created, and perhaps one of the first corporate wellness programs of its kind in the country, has had a tremendous impact on his thriving business. Employees stay for life, enjoying the supportive ecosystem that allows them to grow and thrive personally and professionally.

Dave found that the practices informed his ability to be a better boss, partner, husband, and father. He believed that relationships were key to the success of the organization and the well-being of the people within it. Creating a dynamic that fostered candor and innovation was important to him, so he was willing to invest resources to create a safe and inspired workplace.

Pursuing our own growth and development through relationships enables us to find and show up as the best version of ourselves. In the process of learning to forgive ourselves, tolerate our own imperfections, and show compassion to ourselves, we build that muscle to show the same to others. Dave built that muscle and then flexed it in the form of his groundbreaking corporate wellness program.

When it comes to relationships, as with all the practices, we start where we are and work with ideas and actions that resonate for us. For example, we may choose to begin by hugging our children more often and intentionally or endeavor to build more intimacy with our partner.

As we move through our exploration of the power of touch and connection as an essential self-care ingredient, we couldn't ignore the impact the digital world has on our relationships and the importance of unplugging.

Chapter Eleven

PLUGGING IN AND UNPLUGGING

"I don't know how to get out of this," Ethan said. "I have it all, but I'm not happy. I think I need to start meditating."

Ethan's zip code told me that he'd reached a certain level of success attained by few, but my intuition told me that he faced the same problem I see in a lot of my clients: he woke up at 5 a.m. every day, chugged down a cup of coffee, dictated several emails during his brisk ten-minute walk to the train station, wrote more emails during the thirty-three-minute train ride to midtown Manhattan, and spent the next ten hours in his corner office with his eyes glued to the computer screen or on calls, barely noticing that he could see the Empire State Building from his window. At the end of the day, he repeated his commute in reverse, kissed his wife and children, had a glass or two of wine, watched a mindless Netflix series, and went to bed so he could do the same thing the next day. A nagging voice in the back of Ethan's mind whispered, *Is this all there is? When does my life begin?* While his life looked extraordinary from the outside, with a gorgeous home in the suburbs, a beautiful wife and children, and an extremely high-paying job, he experienced a feeling of inner mediocrity.

I believed I could help Ethan find greater fulfillment, but we had some work to do. Meditation would be only one part of the plan, as I believed that consistent movement and exercise was going to be key in supporting his ability to find stillness. In our first conversation, I mentioned the other three pillars of our program and how different forms of self-care feed off and support each other.

With all my clients, I gather information during our calls, and much like therapy, I ask the questions that help clients find their own answers. I also offer insights and recommendations based on years of study and supporting people in finding greater balance. That said, we are all on our own time lines for personal growth and development, so I can offer information, but I ultimately meet clients where they are and build a trusted partnership from there.

Ethan wanted to meditate. He wasn't interested in

moving more, eating better, or having weekly massages yet. He wasn't quite ready to let go of his behavior patterns—patterns that had served him well professionally, or so he thought. I agreed to meet him where he was. I sent a meditation teacher to his home, and his self-care journey began.

The antidote to overindulging in technology is to be proactive in creating healthy habits to replace those that consume our attention and waste our time. First and foremost, we must approach our relationship with technology with mindfulness and compassion for ourselves—and check our shame at the door as most of us are struggling and working on getting better in this area of our life.

PICTURE-PERFECT MAY NOT BE

Lisa Mason's life looks perfect—on Instagram. Her popular millennial mom feed belies the postpartum depression she suffered after her son was born. With every picture-perfect post, she missed out on living another moment in the pain and bliss of being a new mom. She was so distracted by the story line she presented to the world that she wasn't connecting inward or with her baby in a consistent or meaningful way.

Lisa began meditating and practicing yoga because she was given a gift of a Namaste membership. She was open to anything and thought yoga and meditation could be a nice addition to her story line. At our suggestion, she turned off her phone and found herself alone in her own skin. At first it felt a bit disorienting. As she developed more presence in her physical body, mind, and heart, she began to understand that some moments are meant to be moments, not photo ops. She had a lightbulb moment when she realized she deserved to have experiences for herself and that was enough—no one else had to know or approve. She realized that her attention had been out of alignment with her values, and she was a bit bewildered as to how she got there.

Lisa enjoys her hundreds of thousands of followers and influencer status on Instagram. Because she finds creative expression and the joy of connection in these virtual relationships, there's no need to stop. What she realized, though, was that done without mindfulness (as she was at first), she was misplacing her focus much of the time. By integrating a meditation practice, she was able to have a more wakeful relationship to the moment, her child, and her community of followers.

CONSCIOUS AND INTENTIONAL

Technology has changed our world in less than a century. The tools it brings into our lives are extraordinary. I don't recommend becoming a Luddite, but our relationship to the digital world needs to be intentional. Technology becomes problematic when it takes us away from real life, flesh and bone, eyes, heartbeats, and hands. It's all too easy to slip into reactive mode and allow our brains to be manipulated by the barrage of inputs that are sent our way all day. It's a problem when we're lying in bed scrolling through social media instead of having pillow talk with our partner, reading, or stretching.

We must consciously choose when we plug in and when we unplug. We must understand the difference between being digitally connected and being truly connected to people. When we say yes to our phone, we're saying no to the person sitting next to us, and vice versa.

TIME MANAGEMENT

More and more people come to me for virtual wellness coaching—that is, coaching them to integrate some of the practices discussed in this book in a practical way into their lives. These conversations always start with time management. It's no secret that the amount of time in a day is finite. Yet how often do we reach the end of the day asking ourselves, *Where did the day go?* We often forget that time spent doing one thing is time not spent doing another.

Once again, as with the other practices in the pillars of this book, mindfulness is the foundation of how we spend our time. We have to proactively, mindfully integrate movement, stillness, touch, and nourishment into our day-to-day life. To do that, we also have to understand where we're spending our time.

If we ask ourselves how we're going to come up with the time to do the things we want to do, the first place to look is the digital part of our lives. Today, our relationship to our devices robs us of many other relationships and experiences that could be happening. I'm not suggesting we eliminate the digital part of our lives altogether. Instead, I am suggesting we frame it as a problem to solve. Can we explore how to better optimize our relationship to our digital life rather than spending—wasting—time on activities that prevent us from actualizing some of our other goals and intentions?

I understand the paradox here: devices and apps can be a huge help in time management, yet they are often the things that occupy too much of our time. What's the answer?

Organizing our schedule around time blocks can be the first step toward "finding" more hours in the day to do the things we want to do. The world's most ultra-successful people, some of whom I have worked with, have an extremely evolved and disciplined relationship with time and technology. They do not act impulsively. For example, some of the wisest and most efficient people I know and work with dedicate several hours a day in a compartmentalized way to read and respond to emails, instead of checking it all day long. They like to stay caught up and know what's happening on social media, so they block out a certain amount of time each day to check Facebook, Instagram, LinkedIn, and Twitter. They define what they believe is the appropriate amount of time to engage in these activities daily. When the time is blocked on the calendar and the phone isn't in their hand, people are much less tempted to start scrolling the moment they open their eyes because they know they will have their time when it's healthy and right. As my parents used to say, "There is a time and a place." There is no deprivation or disengagement; it's just time spent on purpose.

This type of time management often means changing ingrained, mindless habits into mindful ones. Digital connection can be great fun, but it is also highly, purposefully addictive, as demonstrated in the documentary *Like*. The film was shown at my son's school to educate teenagers about how apps are designed to manipulate them. Software engineers apply AB testing to know whether, for example, a red notification gets a higher response than a blue notification. The apps are designed to engage us and pull us down a digital rabbit hole. Countless designers and user interface people work to figure out how to solicit the desired response from our brains.

In some ways, it's not our fault if we're addicted to social media, the latest television series, or twenty-four-hour news program. Those outlets were built to make us want to stay. To reach a healthy relationship with plugging in and unplugging, we must first understand that the apps are built to entice us to overindulge. Begin to think about one small change as a starting point.

MAKE SPACE

The digital world has removed the spaciousness in our lives. It's easy to make plans by sending a text or group chat, leading to an overscheduled life. What used to be play is now a competition. Children no longer play pickup games on the cul-de-sac but participate in scheduled practices and traveling teams. They're destined to be overscheduled adults.

Technology allows us to share ideas globally and stay in touch with friends and loved ones who live far away. The ability to connect to anyone virtually anywhere in the world has created a global community few imagined even twenty years ago. Connection and community are important for our well-being, *and* plugging in to our life in real time is a vital part of our wellness formula. To have the best experience of ourselves, it's about finding inspired, reasonable boundaries.

My son is dyslexic and one of the most intelligent and creative people I know. He watches YouTube and knows how to do many things as a result, from playing the ukulele to skateboarding, crafting, and cooking, and he listens to audiobooks voraciously. He is able to voice-to-text his written homework—all to show how technology is changing lives for people with disabilities. As much as I love the idea of playing with sticks and stones, when he is on his iPad, he is most often learning in some way. I am grateful that he has this tool to learn, and I have a huge amount of reverence and gratitude for the technology advancements that are changing our lives, and his life. But I have concerns, too.

I have noticed that teens are not out as often, spending time together at parties and public places. It seems they connect online and hang out from home, and quite enjoy this. The result of kids staying home on a Friday night playing video games is that they are not out and about getting hurt or into trouble. In the strangest way, kids are physically safer than they have been in the past, but I worry about their mental and emotional safety. It seems that because they are spending less time face-to-face, they will be less adept at recognizing facial expressions, body language, etc. The bottom line is that our brains are changing and there is a lot unknown.

Technology clearly has powerful gifts as well as real liabilities. Owning our own mind and choosing where we put our attention and when is the goal. As we think about adding practices from the four pillars into our life to create a wellness plan, it's important to think about how we can control technology and use our time wisely, rather than letting it control us.

The idea of a digital sunset is as simple as turning off our phone and putting it in a drawer at a set hour every evening—after 9 p.m., for example. When we say no to our devices, we can say yes to other fulfilling activities.

THE FOURTH PILLAR: TOUCH
QUESTIONS TO CONSIDER

- How often do you physically connect with other people during the day? Are there moments to integrate additional safe, appropriate touch or affection?
- Have you ever considered a preventative massage? Or thought about booking a consistent monthly (or more) appointment to check in with your body?
- If you have a partner, do you make love regularly? If not, do you wish you did? What would need to shift to find greater fulfillment in this area of your life?
- Where are you resting your eyes and attention? Is it in alignment with how you really feel?
- When was the last time you held hands with someone as you walked?

- Can you frame your most challenging relationships as your teachers? How does that make you feel?
- Do you feel you engage in social media too much, not enough, or just the right amount?

PRACTICES

- Book a style of massage that you have never experienced before. Perhaps a Shiatsu treatment or Thai bodywork? With each experience, even those we don't fully resonate with, we learn something.
- Invest in a beautiful oil or cream and explore self-massage on your abdomen, shoulders, face, or jaw before bed for a week. Just a few minutes can impact your ability to fall asleep feeling full.
- Commit to a digital sunset for one week. Pick a spot for your phone to live at night, and put an auto-response on if you feel anxious about disconnecting. How will that make you feel?
- Experiment with time-blocking an hour in the morning and an hour in the afternoon for email checking, and notice how it impacts your productivity and overall sense of connection to other areas of your work and life.
- Next time you feel a true connection with someone, offer a hug and see how that feels.

CONCLUSION

We are human people living in human bodies. We need to move and be still, we need nourishment and touch, and the practices outlined here certainly help us on a practical level. It's what's between the lines of these practices, the energy of self-care, of loving ourselves, of being in our own skin, that actually makes people happy. The practices can be a vehicle to getting in between those lines.

Actions lead to consequences, and everything we do will take us on a journey. Our obstacles and challenges are part of that journey, too. Through personal ownership, honesty, and vulnerability, we can make our way to the choices that are in alignment with the life that we want to live. And it's okay if it's a bit of a mess sometimes. The universal principles and framework of the four pillars are meant to help us straighten up and play with balance. Balance is a moving target, and there is an inevitable ebb and flow.

This constant movement is the giving and receiving, the joy and pain, the inhale and the exhale, the expansion and contraction, the gazing in and connecting out, and the strength and softness. There's wisdom from within ourselves and receptivity to wisdom from the universe. When it's rooted in mindfulness, we make our way through the four pillars, fostering equilibrium, flow, and abundance through the practices.

Self-care isn't another opportunity for us to be hard on ourselves or feel like we have one more thing on our to-do list. It ultimately enables us to offer our unique gifts more fully to the world, help others, and find grace. We're no longer practicing self-care for external approval or a perfect body or mind, but in honor of ourselves and our relationship with the world around us.

SURRENDER

We work with many golfers because they often have performance anxiety when they step onto the golf course. Our yoga and meditation teachers train them in breath, meditation, and posture within the context of their golf game. One day in conversation with a wonderful friend of mine—an amazing golfer—I said I was going to work with another golfer who had performance anxiety. My friend said, "Oh, that's simple. Just tell him he has to give less shits about it."

His definition of "giving less shits" is my definition of surrender. The bottom line is that yes, we need to do the practices within the four pillars, and we want to optimize as human beings. We also have to let go. The tools give our minds and bodies something to focus on. They help us release the anxiety, tension, and stress of our daily lives—but underneath all of these pillars is the formidable yet worthwhile challenge of letting go of perfection and control.

Cultivating an awakened heart through these practices within the four pillars enables us to engage more fully and authentically in our own life and the world around us. If there's a goal, that's the goal. We need to do the work; otherwise, it's too risky to open our hearts.

We can work in a physical way, through the practice of asana, to open the heart space. When we use yoga postures to open our upper back and shoulders and widen our collarbone, we begin to create a physical pattern in the body that represents an open heart. The physical practice of yoga helps us flush the energy in our body on a regular basis. Other movement practices flush the body, too—think of the runner's high. From the energy of movement, we move into stillness, mindfulness, and space for reflection. We learn to be present in our lives. The energy of stillness connects us to our experience, enabling us to tap into the heart space that was opened through movement. Nourishment feeds us, which enables us to love and give actively because we can't give from a place of fatigue or depletion. Touch reflects the connection we feel with ourselves and others. The practices lead us to work through fear, anger, sadness, and all the things that force us to put up armor. As we peel away the layers, we can appreciate and see the world through sweeter eyes.

The sea of wellness and the ways you can take care of yourself is vast. The language can be overwhelming. Where do you even begin? I suggest that you begin by trusting the wisdom of your own path. I'm hoping this book has provided a framework for you to think about the different ingredients that will help you explore that path with curiosity, patience, and joy.

ACKNOWLEDGMENTS

Life is a team game. This book was written by my team, channeled through me, with the help of a village. The learnings, teachings, and offerings in this book began in my early childhood, where I am grateful to my late grandparents, particularly Elaine Dretler, whose voice I hear in my head almost daily. I thank my magnificent parents, Bobbie and John Dretler, whose love, support, and daily help enable my work and family to survive and thrive. Their words and wisdom are on every page, and I can't believe I was lucky enough to be born as their daughter.

My brother Adam Dretler, who was my first student, friend, listener, and believer in me—your earnest love, loyalty, and support is a rock in my life.

I thank Jeffrey Wald, my brother-by-law, but so much more—a friend, advisor, supporter, and reminder of what it means to live fully, grow, and give with enormous generosity on every level. Thank you for helping me bring this book to the world and in turn hopefully help others.

My in-laws, Phyllis and William Wald—your unconditional love and unwavering support is a gift and a vital part of the foundation that makes our work and our life possible.

I am so grateful to Julie Dretler and Rachel and Adam Wald for your loving friendship and support, and for sharing so many nourishing moments together as a family, which informs my work and play, and nurtures my children, Michael, and me.

I also thank Danielle Mossé, my dear friend and soul sister, whose voice is woven through mine in these writings and in the work I do every day. Your wisdom and love is my source, consistently.

This book was inspired and made possible by my incredible, loyal students and clients of Namaste New York, who have also been my teachers and some of my closest friends for the past twenty years. Working with you and learning from your greatness, intelligence, and openness has inspired me, filled me up, and given me purpose. Thank you for trusting me and enabling me to make a living doing something I find so deeply fulfilling. You know who you are, and I love you. Some of you have also invested in Namaste in a concrete way, which was the hardest thing I ever asked for and has enabled Namaste to touch more lives and help more people. I am humbly grateful.

To my many gifted personal teachers, doctors, healers, and therapists since I began this journey almost thirty years ago—you have mirrored back the importance of this work, and enabled me to find sparks of divine wisdom within myself. I'm grateful for your teachings and reflection, and in some ways I feel we are just beginning.

I hold total and complete appreciation for the team of gifted writers, editors, and project managers who have enabled me to bring this book to fruition amidst my very full life. You are genius.

And to the extraordinary team of builders and wellness professionals at Namaste New York, who hustle to help and cultivate healing on a daily basis—you are an army of lightworkers, and together we are making leaders better people, bringing healing to the sick, and having some fun along the way.

And last but most importantly, I would like to acknowledge Michael, Jonah, Eli, and Eviana—my husband and business partner, and my three children, who live with me every day and bear witness to my own journey, filled with trials and tribulations, toward wholeness and ease. We teach best what we are learning ourselves, and I am learning every moment of every day. Michael, I am forever grateful for your patience, your belief in me, your tireless support, and of course your amazing humor. This work and these teachings and learnings are *ours*, born out of us. You and the children are my gifts and teachers, and I love you.

ABOUT THE AUTHOR

A wellness practitioner for over twenty-five years, **JULIE WALD** is the founder, CEO, and Chief Wellness Officer at Namaste New York. She holds a master's degree in social work from New York University. Julie began her career in 1995 as a clinical social worker treating adults, children, and adolescents in inpatient and outpatient mental health settings. In the process of building her impressive mental health practice, Julie also pursued her personal wellness objectives and in doing so became a Certified Yoga Instructor, Meditation Teacher, Thai Bodyworker, and Reiki Master. The mastery of these disciplines combined with an intense fascination for Eastern wisdom have proven to be invaluable assets to her professional path.

Namaste New York was conceived in the wake of the attacks of September 11, 2001. While working as a clinical social worker and moonlighting as a yoga and meditation teacher in the homes of prominent New Yorkers, Julie noticed a profound shift in how individuals search for personal connections and meaningful practices to nourish their mind, body, and spirit. She observed the acute challenges people face to find the approach, practices, and practitioners to accommodate their needs and busy schedules. In response to this, Julie and her husband, Michael, created Namaste New York as a wellness company that is uniquely positioned to advise, coach, curate, and deliver wellness to individuals, families, and organizations.

Today, Namaste New York serves a vast and influential clientele of high-performing business leaders and celebrities in achieving their health and wellness goals, as well as people coping with acute and chronic illness who want to leverage the power of evidence-based wellness practices on their journey. As Namaste's Chief Wellness Advisor, Julie guides her team to help clients cultivate lifelong well-being through extraordinary self-care planning and practices.

An unwavering commitment to service has always been central to Julie's personal ethos. In addition to serving clients, Namaste delivers complementary wellness treatments to a wide variety of underserved and disenfranchised people in New York schools, hospitals, and other organizations.